The Lure of

TO STEVE.

PUBLISHED AND PRINTED BY
S. & L. PRINTERS.
36 GLENVILLE ROAD, WALKFORD,
CHRISTCHURCH, DORSET.

FIRST PUBLISHED MARCH 1994
RE-ISSUED NOVEMBER 1995

CONTENTS

PREFACE.

My father was an officer in the Royal Air Force during the Second World War. His love of aviation naturally indoctrinated me into the world of aircraft in my younger years and even now, thirty years later, I still feel compelled to run out of the house if I hear an overflying aircraft.

The untimely death of my father meant that his house had to be sorted out and any would-be heirlooms distributed between the children. I was surprised to find in the loft the remains of a 1/12th scale rubber band aeroplane that he had made for me back in 1965.

It was in great need of refurbishment but aided by a new set of plans which remarkably were still available, the restoration was fairly easy to complete. Painted in very non-standard bright yellow, and bearing the equally non-standard registration G-WAHS, my father's initials (it bore G-AROB before the restoration) it was a great moment when it was tied in its final resting place, hanging from the conservatory ceiling.

The garden of our house plays host to an unruly laurel hedge. It too clearly needed some restoration back in the summer of 1992 and I was grateful that a cricketing friend recommended his father as a suitable restorer of all things flora.

Having restored the hedge and whilst drinking one of my beers, mention was made of the yellow aeroplane hanging from the ceiling.

"Am I right, is it a Fairchild Argus?" he asked.

"Quite correct." I replied, "How did you know that?"

The reason that Les White knew this relatively unusual aircraft is basically the book you are about to read.

At a New Year party in 1992/3, Les (whilst drinking more of my beers) became quite engrossed in two books about the R.A.F. and New Forest aerodromes. He borrowed one of them and when he returned it he also gave me the draft manuscript of a book to read through. I read it, enjoyed it and now you can too .... so read on and savour some aviation nostalgia.

ROB SAWYER, WALKFORD, DORSET.

23/8/40

New Milton.

West side of Station Road, north of traffic lights.

1/11/93

Original photographs of bombing on display in the New Milton Memorial Centre.

INTRODUCTION.

In October 1984 I was aboard a Boeing 737 travelling to Rome at around 500 m.p.h.. The altitude was something above 30,000ft. as we crossed the Alps and looking out at those majestic peaks, I realised in a moment of revelation what a privilege I was enjoying. For thousands of years men had looked upwards; and in more recent times had climbed upwards to scale those very mountains upon which I gazed. They had sacrificed life and limb, suffered the agonies inflicted by sub-zero temperatures, ice, snow and lack of oxygen and there was I, sipping a drink and lounging in shirtsleeved luxury within my high-technology cocoon ---- looking down!

My father was born before the Wright Brothers won their battle against gravity for the first time and lived to watch men walking upon the Moon in his own fireside armchair as it actually happened. Any wonder that I should marvel at the great adventure in the sky which had, as it were, unfolded before my very eyes?

Looking back, my love affair with the aeroplane started in earnest during the Battle of Britain, when knowing friend from foe was a matter of self-preservation, well illustrated by the topical joke, "Famous last words ---- It's one of ours!"

Since that time aeroplanes have held a fascination for me which has persisted to this day and even now, more than half a century later, with all the complications of a full and busy life, my eyes automatically turn to the skies at the sound of aero-engines.

My wife and I were recently invited to a friend's party. Quite by chance he showed me a book dealing with the wartime airfields of the New Forest and immediately I was transported back in time. I was there again, watching the Thunderbolts forming up before setting off to beat hell out of "Fortress Europe" just prior to D-Day; watching the wing-tip vortices of a Beaufighter form and die as it pulled around in a "splitarse" turn at 500ft.; at 5,000ft, over the Hampshire countryside sitting at the controls of a Curtiss Commando; ducking instinctively as a Mosquito roared out of nowhere at treetop height ----- . That night my memories refused to let me sleep.

I had often contemplated writing on the subject; now it became imperative! In so far as my memory serves me and with the aid of a few glances at the appropriate records to help with technical details and dates, the following is an entirely authentic (though somewhat digressive) narrative.

CHAPTER 1
STRAWS IN THE WIND.

My earliest recollection of aeroplanes is of a single engined biplane which landed in Fawcett's field opposite my home in Gore Road, New Milton. I can remember being left behind by the other children as we raced across the field to see the "flying machine". The pilot wore flying helmet and goggles and held something resembling a clipboard in his hand. Why he had landed, whether he took off again or anything else about this thrilling encounter has now drifted out of my memory; but that is not surprising; I could not have been more than seven years old at the time.

Some time later, probably around 1936, I watched several small aircraft all gaily painted in bright colours as they passed over our garden. It was a Sunday morning and the boys next door who were older than me said the planes were going to "The Display". We craned our necks eagerly counting them as they flew gracefully overhead and then gasped with surprise at one which was completely different from the others. It had no proper wings. Instead, in addition to a conventional engine, what appeared to be an oversized propeller rotated above the fuselage in the horizontal plane. That day the word "autogiro" was added to my vocabulary.

I think "The Display" was almost certainly Alan Cobham's flying circus which visited the newly opened Somerford (Christchurch) aerodrome quite often in the Thirties. It may in fact have been based there as Alan Cobham was part owner of the aerodrome previously known as Burry's Meadow after Harold Burry to whom it had belonged. Incidentally he became the commanding officer of 171 (Christchurch) Squadron of the Air Training Corps when it was formed early in the war.

On a later occasion I was fortunate enough to attend one of these marvellous spectacles. Wing walking, inverted flying, parachuting and "looping the loop" entertained and thrilled the large crowd, one of whom had to be lifted onto his father's shoulders to see what was happening. I can remember my father complaining of my weight as we watched in wonder from the airfield boundary on Mudeford Lane.

I was in those days an avid collector of cigarette cards. These were much the same as the bubble gum cards which my grandson collects today with equal enthusiasm. On the face of each card was a picture and on the reverse a few words describing the "Film Stars", "Cage Birds" etc. which were issued in a "Series of Fifty". My favourites, maybe a hint of things to come, were "Aeroplanes (Civil)" and "Aircraft of the R.A.F.".

By that time, the last few years of peace, I was able to relate these pictures to the aeroplanes appearing overhead in increasing numbers. One day as I stood upon the cliff at Highcliffe, an R.A.F. plane flew so low along the beach that I was actually able to look down upon it. It was a Fairey Gordon, my first positive identification.

Then there was the "Empire Air Day" which must have been either 1938 or more probably '39. I did not actually attend this event at Somerford but my father did and the two types which became fixed in my mind were the Wellington and Hampden. These names would soon become household words in the early days of Bomber Command's offensive against the Third Reich. There had been rumours among my friends that there would be a thousand planes in attendance, but I had read that most of the aerodromes were opening to the public so thought it unlikely. Knowing what I know now, it is a wonder that there were enough planes to make a reasonable showing let alone anything on that scale!

In the Autumn of 1938, just after the "Munich Crisis" when war appeared to have been averted (but not for long) gas masks had been issued to the general public and "Air Raid Precautions" appeared in my "fag cards". I heard the first wailing of the New Milton air raid siren when it was tested about that time and by then grown-ups were talking about "when" rather than "if".

At school in the playground (on the corner of Gore and Vincent roads and many years since re-developed for housing) we all became puzzled one day by long looping white trails in the sky, dramatic against the blue. Mr. Brooks, one of our teachers told us they were being made by fighter planes which would be our protection from German bombers which had proved so shatteringly effective in the Spanish Civil War. For the next few days the playground was filled by boys with outstretched arms zooming around and "machine-gunning" everything in sight; especially the girls!

At ten years of age I was reading the News Chronicle, the daily newspaper taken by my parents and had a childishly fair idea of what was going on in the world. There seemed little doubt that a man called Herr Hitler was going to make the same mistake as the Kaiser in 1914 and take on The British Empire. Well, we had beaten the Germans that time and we should undoubtedly beat them again, particularly as we had the best aeroplanes in the world; everybody said so!

CHAPTER 2
THE AWAKENING

On the third day of September 1939 the inevitable happened; we were at war. The wireless was eagerly listened to but the massive air raids that were expected at the onset of hostilities failed to materialise and the skies above New Milton saw little change as the so called "Phoney War" continued until the Spring of 1940. We had heard a few "alerts" but seen nothing of the Luftwaffe.

However, more R.A.F. planes were arriving on the scene, including some from the Special Duties Flight at Somerford of which I knew nothing at the time. I now know it operated in conjunction with the A.D.E.E. (Air Defence Experimental Establishment) on the highly secret testing and development of radio and "radiolocation" (soon to be renamed "radar") equipment. Flying trials were carried out from late April 1940 with such aircraft types as the Hurricane, Harrow, Battle, Anson and Blenheim and at a later stage, the small airfield at Sway was constructed as a dispersal station but closed in December 1941. It seems possible that the enemy had some inkling of the work connected with Sway as it was bombed several times in it's short life of about sixteen months.

I have had to wait fifty three years to hear of the Swordfish which crashed in a field to the east of Stem Lane, less that half a mile from where I lived! This incident occurred in April 1940 and I had no recollection of it whatsoever!

In the early days of 1940 some of my friends who had been evacuated from Southampton were beginning to take notes of the aircraft they saw and if we stood upon the parapet of the railway bridge at Stem Lane, something strictly forbidden by our parents, several large barrage balloons over the city and docks were clearly visible.

A biplane, probably an Audax, towing a drogue target shaped like an oversized windsock was seen occasionally and a Battle in the half black, half white day/night camouflage often appeared flying on a patrol parallel to the coast. This was the time when I saw my first Sunderland flying boat.

Air raid precautions in the still relatively peaceful "calm before the storm" were not taken seriously by anyone in our locality except Mr Philips the Air Raid Warden. I can recall him earnestly acclaiming the merits of the "stirrup pump", a hand-held spray to be used to extinguish a small fire. The insignificant jet of water it produced drew the inevitable scoffing comment from my Grandfather White that he could piddle better than that and a fine old argument ensued. In order to prove his point, Mr Philips organised a demonstration in Edgar's field nearby, the following Sunday morning and accompanied by a colleague complete with an armband and steel helmut labelled with a "W" (Warden), lit a small fire. The colleague got off to a poor start by slopping the water over himself as the bucket tipped while climbing through the rails of the fence, (typical "Dad's Army" stuff!) delighting the twenty or onlookers, mostly intent on taking the mickey.

As the demonstration got under way a Whitley flew low overhead and seizing the opportunity to bring home the seriousness of the situation he asked pompously, "If that was an enemy bomber, what would you do?" Jack Hall, a lad of about sixteen and always a ready wit replied, "Do a bloody bunk!". I cannot remember if the fire was extinguished or not.

That was the way things were before the war came to our doorstep and although the stirrup pump proved to be an excellent appliance it was ever after remembered in our family lore as an object of fun.

But we were soon to be forced to take matters seriously. In May the dam burst and Hitler's Panzers poured across The Low Countries and Northern France. Almost nightly then the siren would drive us from our beds to huddle miserably at the foot of the stairs (reckoned to be the safest place in the house) waiting fearfully for the drone of aero-engines. Sometimes they came, but mostly we would wait patiently for the "all clear" to sound and tumble back into bed without hearing a thing. On several occasions, no sooner had we got to sleep than "Wailing Winnie" would drag us out again. Needless to say, my father and grandfather soon refused to get up at all but the rest of us did.

One night during an "alert" a German bomber's characteristic uneven drone was heard and it appeared that the plane was circling as the noise failed to fade in the way that it normally did. A few hundred yards up the road from our house stood a large gasometer and my grandmother was convinced that this was the target. The droning continued for some time and then stopped abruptly and after a few moment's silence resumed. It certainly had us guessing until my mother started to chuckle. "That's Dad snoring", she said and we all exploded into laughter, exaggerated by the relief we felt.

Although we had moments of light relief, the certainty of knowing that something was bound to happen sooner or later and not knowing quite what it would be, put a strain on everyone; and then we had our first bomb. It dropped in "Fifty Acres" a field at Walkford Farm. The following Sunday we all trooped off to see the crater which turned out to be eight or nine feet across and four deep.

I believe this was about the time I saw a Red Cross hospital train taking some of the survivors of Dunkirk to recuperate in the West Country. Many of the blinds were drawn and vague khaki figures were visible at the open windows and I was afraid.

Then the "invasion scare" started. Our house on the corner of Stem Lane was designated a "gun house" and a pit was dug in the front garden by the L.D.V. (Local Defence Volunteers) later to become the Home Guard. The pit we were informed, was to accommodate another gun. This annoyed my grandfather intensely. As he said, they only had one rifle between four men, so where were all the heavier guns to come from? Added to this, the officer in charge was classed by Grandad as a "jumped-up little fart"; and the fact that he had ruined the front garden didn't help!

Even if there were no guns there certainly appeared to be plenty of barbed wire. Coil upon coil of it was slung around the network of slit trenches which seemed to appear overnight and obsolete farm implements were moved to the railway bridges which were all drilled ready for demolition. Anything to hold up the expected advance of the "Jerries" when they arrived as we firmly expected they would. Telegraph poles were erected in all the larger fields to deter glider landings. Empty tar barrels buried horizontally in the roadside banks enabled a man to shoot through a hole in the bottom into the road from cover, whilst others, filled with any inflammable liquid available were positioned so that they could be rolled downhill and ignited against an enemy vehicle.

In the event, the R.A.F. defended us exactly as Mr. Brooks had said that they would and thankfully the ramshackle defences were never put to the test.

Somewhere around this time, before The Battle of Britain commenced in July, I had the most remarkable stroke of good fortune. I acquired a Penguin paperback entitled "Aircraft Recognition" by R.A. Saville-Sneath. It contained silhouettes of all the important British and German aircraft in plan, side and end elevations. Gold, pure gold! The main distinguishing features were listed as wings, engines, tail, fuselage, undercarriage and radiators (or rarities), reduced to WETFUR, the easily remembered acronym.

For a couple of days nothing else mattered. Either alone or with friends I practised and practised until I could name every aircraft in every elevation. From that time on it became a matter of honour to recognise every aircraft seen; and there were more now of more varied types.

Well, whatever others felt, I for one was ready for the Luftwaffe!

There was not long to wait! By early August the siren was sounding so often that, particularly by night, we took little notice. School holidays were on by this time and we were "spotting" all the time.

On Sunday 11th August, I was helping my father to pick peas at our allotment in Walkford Road. There had been some firing out to sea and then, taking us completely by surprise, a plane roared out of an apparently empty sky diving straight at us, literally about thirty feet above the ground. There was no time for hesitation. Dad threw himself at me and the next thing I knew I was lying on the ground among the broken pea sticks, gasping under his weight as he sprawled across me in an endeavour to protect me from the expected bullets. But no bullets came. Instead we heard a grinding thud as the aircraft skidded and bumped to a halt, belly-landing in the field across the railway line, that same "Fifty Acres", only a few yards from the patch of bare earth which denoted the site of the recently filled crater.

Jumping to our feet, we raced to the railway, scrambled down the steep embankment, across the rails and up the other side. Breathless from a mixture of fear, excitement and physical exertion, we pulled ourselves over the bank to behold a Hurricane, resting upon its underside with a broken propeller and damage to its fuselage and port wing. "Robbie" Robins, a farm worker was cutting at the pilot's harness and as we approached, dragged him half conscious from the cockpit. There was nothing Dad or I could do but stare as we stood panting and trying to regain our breath.

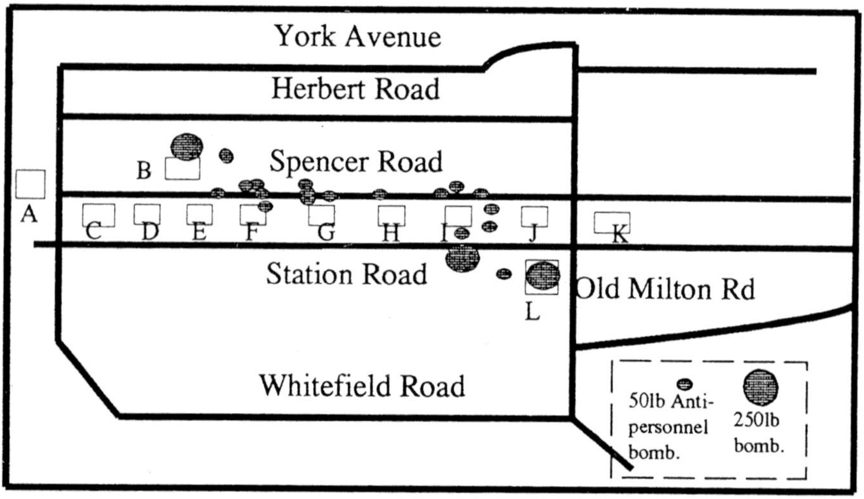

Diagram of the bombing of New Milton.
A. Water Tower: B. White Cottage, Dr Dawn: C. Essenden: D. Council Offices: E. Oakfield, G Lane: F. Turnberry Dr Wallace: G. Kingsley Dr Devereaux: H. Rockfield, Dr Caldwell: I. James (Lawyers): J. Nat Provincial Bank: K. Westminster Bank: L. Roberts Adlards.

The pilot soon recovered from his bang on the head and was delighted to learn that he was within a mile of Highcliffe where an aunt of his lived in Stuart Road. H's damaged fighter was salvaged a short time later, the wings being removed and stacked together with the fuselage on the bed of a "Queen Mary", one of the sixty foot long transporters named after the famous transatlantic liner.

In the early evening of 23rd August, a friend Phil Breaker and I were walking in Gore Road near the top of the hill. Hearing engines, we looked up and saw coming towards us a Junkers 88. This was the first German plane I had identified with certainty although there had been several suspects. It passed over us at medium height, veered to the West and then was lost to sight.

After about fifteen minutes we had arrived at Phil's house on the Walkford side of the brook and heard several explosions from the direction of New Milton. Running to the railway bank, we looked up the line and saw smoke and flames. I lived in that direction and full of fear, sprinted off as fast as I could. My home was safe; the fire was further up the road.

My mother, who had actually observed the bombs falling, refused to let me go and see what had happened. It was as well; Station Road, New Milton was in ruins and Archie Bursey and Barbara Green, my schoolfriends, were dead and so was Bill Pitman a neighbour. In addition, another friend, Ivan Briant and our old headmaster from the Junior School, "Skip" Barker, were seriously injured. In all twenty-four lives were lost that day and the damage was unbelievable. There was however one tiny compensation. All the boys managed to get a piece of shrapnel as a souvenir!

I think that was the time that my feelings of a need for revenge began to crystallise. I was nearly twelve years old and reasoned that maybe if the war lasted long enough, I would be able to fly a plane and drop bombs on Germany.

The major air battle in those memorable summer skies was spreading westward from Kent and Sussex and as September opened there was enemy activity every day.

One afternoon whilst feeding the chickens I heard distant firing and looking towards the Isle of Wight saw a Stuka (Junkers 87 dive bomber) plummeting down trailing smoke. Sometimes smoke canisters were carried by the German planes, their contents being released in order to simulate damage thus enabling them to escape, so what appeared to me to be another victory for Fighter Command may well have been nothing more than a routine attempt to avoid farther combat. Nevertheless I felt a glow of satisfaction at the sight.

On the afternoon of Sunday 15th September, at the height of the struggle for supremacy of the air and later to be immortalised as "Battle of Britain Day", my mother, Aunt Annie and myself stood in Glenville Road, Walkford. There was a "dog-fight" in progress over the sea. In as many minutes, we saw three planes shot down, one breaking up in what, because of the distance, appeared to be quite a leisurely manner.

Before the mighty trial of strength drew to a close I was again witness to an incident which, although it literally lasted only two seconds, is as clear in my mind now as it was on that afternoon at Ashley Senior School. The siren had not sounded, but suddenly, as Class la was composing anthologies, there was the stutter of machine-gun fire and the roar of engines very low over the school.

Outside the classroom windows, blast walls had been erected and it was just possible to see the sky by peering up at an angle from where I sat. Into this narrow band of blue plunged a blazing Junkers 88. I leaped excitedly onto the top of my desk yelling, "It's a bloody Jerry and he's all on fire!" I was rebuked by Miss McLeod but I cannot now remember whether it was on account of my language or my actions.

The unfortunate bomber crashed on Hordle Cliffs and the crew, all dead, were recovered and buried in New Milton churchyard where they remained for several years before being taken back to Germany and laid to rest in their native land. (I believe, although there is a possibility that their remains now lay in the central German war cemetery in Staffordshire.)

Every day during the battle, from the middle of July until the end of October, when the fighting petered out due to bad weather and mutual exhaustion, I recorded the losses of aircraft, friend and foe. On that Sunday when we had watched the culmination of Hitler's gigantic air offensive being routed it was officially announced that one hundred and eighty seven enemy planes bad been destroyed.

We know now that our own propaganda machine was no less unscrupulous than that of the infamous Dr. Goebbels and that many of the figures released were considerably inflated when it came to the number of raiders "downed". Even so Goering's much vaunted Luftwaffe had indeed taken sufficient of a mauling to deter Hitler from launching his planned invasion.

The first incendiary bombs to be dropped locally came down one night that winter, one landing by extraordinary coincidence in "Fifty Acres" near the searchlight site which had been established just over the railway bridge where Wyndham Road leads into the fields.

These bombs were relatively very small weighing only about two kilos but dropped in the vicinity of any combustible material were capable of starting a fire. In this instance, the only evidence remaining was a patch of scorched earth about the size of a dustbin lid. The metal tailfin, highly prized by young collectors of such items, had vanished long before I came upon the scene and my hopes of adding to my collection of army badges, cartridge cases, shrapnel and the like were dashed to the ground.

Prior to the war a network of so called "Shadow Factories" was envisaged as part of the re-armament programme which sought to expand and re-equip the RA.F. One of these was the Airspeed works at Somerford, situated between the airfield and the main road out of Christchurch to the East. Production of the Oxford, destined to become the most numerous twin-engined British trainer of the war years, commenced there at the end of 1940.

Painted in the standard colour scheme for trainers of the day with yellow under-surfaces and "sand aid spinach" camouflage above, they became an everyday sight.

Inevitably there were crashes and a local depot was set up at the commandeered "Wall and Martin" garage (now "Olympian") at the north end of Barton Court Avenue in New Milton to recover them. Once received, the "Oxboxes" were reduced to re-usable spares as far as the damage would allow. Sadly, anyone employed at "Wall and Martin's" at that time will recall that there was always plenty of work.

One such crash occurred sometime I believe in 1942. At any event, my mother was working as a domestic servant at a house in Marley Avenue. The bungalow estate which exists now in that area was in those days "Stem Lane Copse", a tract of ancient woodland, oak trees underplanted with hazel in the traditional style.

In the heavy morning fog there was the sound of engines and then a splintering crash which was heard by my mother from where she worked about two hundred yards away. Running quickly to the scene she saw an Oxford perched in the trees several feet from the ground. I cannot now remember the details of what happened other than that none of the crew were killed and that Mum was first on the scene and helped in the rescue.

As soon as I heard the news I raced off on my bike to see the crash which was quite spectacular. Before long of course, the plane had been salvaged and was soon on the way to "Wall and Martin's" to join its unfortunate fellows.

That same month that the first Oxford took to the air from Somerford, Southampton suffered a truly terrible ordeal at the hands of Goering's Luftwaffe.

Unable to achieve his desire for mastery of the skies above Britain, he sought to bomb us into submission by devastating night attacks upon our major cities and ports.

We had watched in dismay as three barrage balloons fell blazing to the ground one day in the summer, but at twenty miles away in daylight there was nothing else we could see. How different it was by night; and what a show to behold! The oddly nicknamed "Flaming Onions", in reality tracer shells, arced lazily into the darkness tearing it apart in great upward slashes of greenish orange light whilst the long searchlight beams probed the blackness wandering hither and thither to the accompaniment of flashes from exploding bombs and shells. Sometimes a flare with its parachute clearly visible in the magnesium glare would attract the attention of the ground gunners and coloured Very lights would loop across the vast glow of the burning city and the decoy fires lit in deserted areas of countryside where bombing would be harmless.

Instead of cowering indoors as we had done in the early days, we now regularly met our neighbours at the back fence when "Jerry" was about. There was no question of dressing and undressing, we slept in our clothes just in case; so when things began to get noisy we went straight out, curiosity overcoming caution.

Sometimes an aircraft would show up silver when caught in the beam of a searchlight and as it manoeuvred to free itself from the clawing illumination, other beams would "cone" upon it. There was always speculation amongst us as to whether or not the beams would succeed in holding a victim for sufficient time to range the "Ack Ack" (Anti-aircraft guns) but almost invariably the evasive tactics enabled the enemy to escape.

On one of the rare occasions when the gunners could see what they were shooting at they scored a direct hit and the luckless raider burst into flames. As it descended part of the wreckage tore itself from the rest and the two flaming sections descended slowly as we watched in awed silence. Suddenly, the spell broken, I cheered and the men clapped. (Looking back, it seems a mild response, somewhat on a par with applauding a catch at a cricket match, but half a century ago we had not been exposed to television where over-reaction is the norm.) My mother and grandmother were even less demonstrative remaining silent until Nan said sadly "Don't cheer. That's some poor mothers' sons." Her voice was choking and I am sure that had there been enough light we would have seen tears in her eyes.

Whilst chatting to Richard Reeves, a fellow enthusiast of wartime aviation matters during the preparation of this book, I discovered that this incident resulted in the remains of the Heinkel 111 crashing at Pilley, north of Lymington. A school friend of mine, Tony Long was helping on his father's farm nearby (but several weeks later) when amongst the standing corn he discovered the semi-decomposed body of a German airman, one of the crew. Strangely enough, I had heard of this discovery at the time but it has taken over fifty years to discover that the two incidents are linked!

I learned something the night that poor mother's son and his comrades died. Until then I had always thought of the R.A.F. aircrews as "our courageous airmen" and the enemy as "murdering "Jerries"", or as Nan used to refer to them, "They baggerin' o' jerrypots". Now I began to realise the wretchedly evil immorality of war in a way that had never hitherto occurred to me. What we had witnessed in the sky that night was merely the tip of a great iceberg of suffering and woe to be multiplied many millions of times in the succeeding years.

But to be honest, there was precious little compassion for the enemy in my mind at that time. I was learning everything I could about aeroplanes so that one day I could fly a bomber over Germany and personally give them a dose of their own medicine. I wanted to fly, to fight, to kill and maim; to avenge my friends and my country. Such was my youthful and simplistic ambition in the darkest days of that most terrible of wars.

To add to all the misery of that hellish winter the weather heaped even more difficulty and discomfort upon those whose homes had been destroyed or rendered uninhabitable. Snow, freezing rain and plunging temperatures were more in evidence than not. However, many of the Southampton "Bombed-outs" found sanctuary in New Milton. Some settled there permanently and quite a number of today's Miltonians have their roots in the Southampton of pre-blitz days.

When the first party arrived, they were accommodated in our school so we had a couple of days holiday until they could be found somewhere to live. The boys all wore American "lumber jackets" and probably the best and warmest long trousers they had ever possessed. We local lads were quite jealous of these fine clothes, so much better than our own and it took some time for the fact to sink in that had it not been for the generosity of our friends across the Atlantic and their "Bundles for Britain", many would have been utterly destitute.

For some time an "us and them" situation reigned in the school playground but gradually these unfortunate children and others like them from Portsmouth which had also been heavily bombed, became integrated into our country style of life.

In retrospect of course, the terrible ordeals of bombing suffered in Britain were but a pale shadow of the plight of Germany in the later stages of the war when for example, Dresden was virtually erased from the map in a few hours. In that vast firestorm created by over seven hundred R.A.F. Lancasters more than one in ten of its half-million population were killed on the night of 13th February 1945, substantially in excess of the number of immediate deaths at Hiroshima when the first atomic bomb heralded a new age.

At the time of the bombing of Rotterdam by the Germans in the Spring of 1940 the easterly wind had conveyed a hint of what was happening there as far as New Milton. A faint yet definite stink of burnt oil was in evidence and it could have been no coincidence that a few days earlier, Europe's largest oil refinery and storage complex was almost completely destroyed.

Likewise at Southampton in the "Blitz". This time however it was not oil but foodstuffs. A giant warehouse containing fats and meat under refrigeration was set ablaze. I went to my vantage point at Stem Lane railway bridge each morning to see if the cloud of smoke was still issuing from what was then an unknown source and as I recall, it was several days before it had subsided. Although I did not know it at the time, as I watched, firemen with pitifully inadequate resources were battling against rivers of molten butter and fats and the dense acrid smoke they produced.

There must have been many unsung heroes in this and similar situations; just ordinary people doing what had to be done. But my only inkling of this was the pall of smoke up the railway line and the occasional whiff of a sweetish sooty odour.

Only in the context of time and experience can we look back and realise the true horror of those days. They were indeed horrific and yet, because we had no option but to carry on and hope for the best we survived. My Grandad, something of a hard man, scoffed at the "Blitz" pictures of placards saying "Britain Can Take It!" His comment was, "Course we can take it. There ain't nothin' else we can do! We GOT to take it!"

Like a tiny candle flame in the all-pervading gloom of the winter of 1940-41, one incident cheered me tremendously. My father and I were digging in the garden one Sunday morning. A heightening roar of Merlin engines, by that time easily recognisable, approached from inland and looking up we saw a squadron of Hurricanes flying very low in impeccable formation. The sound was deafening and when they had passed over Dad said,"Well, we've still got twelve left!" and I could see the pride glistening in his eyes. He had wanted to serve in the R.A.F. but had failed the medical examination. But I was going to join. Of that I was certain; and as soon as I possibly could!

CHAPTER 3
CONFIRMATION OF AN IDEAL.

The following three years saw a steadily increasing number of aircraft in local skies and also a greater diversity of types. Offensive sweeps over Northern France or "Rhubarbs", reputedly so-called because of their similar effect on the bowels, became the main Fighter Command activity in 1941. Large numbers of fighters, mostly Spitfires, would skim the Channel waters to get below the enemy radar and then fly low over the French countryside, trying to coax or goad the Luftwaffe into combat and strafing their airfields.

This activity took on a special significance after the commencement of "Operation Barbarossa", the German invasion of The U.S.S.R.. Any operations which tied up aircraft in the West bad the indirect effect of relieving pressure on the Russians and at that time, together with the night bombing offensive, this was the only means by which immediate assistance could be rendered.

With the exception of Ibsley, north of Ringwood, none of the local airfields which were to evolve into such a prominent feature of the later war years had as yet become operational, but nevertheless there were always opportunities to 'spot" and largish formations were occasionally seen.

There were plenty of trainers in evidence at this time besides the Oxfords which were now coming off the production lines in a steady flow. Ansons, Tiger Moths, Magisters, Harvards, Masters and Dominies were numerous, forging the increasingly potent weapon which would eventually destroy the Luftwaffe and lay waste vast areas of the once all-powerful Fatherland.

In February 1942 the first of some seven hundred Airspeed Horsa troop carrying assault gliders made its test flight from the factory at Somerford. The lumbering blunt-ended Whitley with its characteristic nose down flying attitude was the usual tug, although the Albemarle, produced by Armstrong Whitworth and rejected as a bomber, was intended to tow the Horsas into battle. Operational requirements dictated otherwise however and their use was limited. Several were later sent to Russia and the Russian crews trained at Hurn, but at what period I am not certain.

Numerous experiments were soon under way to implement the concept of the air transportation of effective numbers of troops and their equipment. One of these was the "double tow" which consisted of one Whitley and two Horsas, not in line astern as the Russians and Germans sometimes operated, but flying in a "V" formation. This rather unlikely configuration which must have called for superlative skills on the part of the glider pilots, particularly in ten-tenths cloud conditions, was soon abandoned in favour of a single tow. Interestingly though, photographs of the Rhine Crossing, the last and by far the most effective of the great airborne enterprises, show American Skytrain (C.47) tugs with two C.G.4a Hadrians apiece using ropes of different lengths.

This technique was also used by the same type of aircraft and gliders in General Wingate's incredible Chindit forays behind the Japanese lines in the Burma campaign. One has to remember though that the Horsa was a considerably larger and heavier craft than its American counterpart. In fact, the Horsa's empty weight, 7,500lbs was exactly the same as that of a fully laden Hadrian and it was also capable of lifting a normal load exceeding its own weight!

Although the Wellington had been the backbone of Bomber Command in the early war years, its place was gradually being taken by the new four-engined trio, the Stirling, Halifax and Lancaster, and at this stage it was decided to carry out tests to determine its suitability as a glider tug. I had in fact seen several examples of the Horsa double tow, but only one of a Wellington. No wonder; it was immediately discovered that because of its construction the Wellington was eminently unsuitable. This twin-engined bomber's designer Barnes Wallis (also of bouncing bomb fame in the breaching of the Ruhr dams) had invented a criss-cross method of airframe manufacture known as the geodetic system. This he had originally used on the Wellesley and later on the Wellington with considerable success as the aerodynamic loading was spread, thus evening out the stresses. Its strength/weight ratio was consequently very high and its ability to absorb battle damage excellent. However when subjected to the longditudinal loads imposed by towing a glider it stretched like an opening trellis! This unfortunate characteristic resulted in splitting of the doped fabric covering and a lengthening of the Wellington's fuselage by several inches! The project was abandoned.

Another failure was the Westland Whirlwind, a most distinctive looking twin-engined fighter with a high tailplane, designed for long range duties and reputed (incorrectly) at the time to have the highest speed of any British fighter of the period. On a few occasions Whirlwinds acted as escorts for medium bomber penetrations of the Ruhr in daylight. They were also tried on "Rhubarbs", but their Peregrine engines proved incapable of living up to expectations and after a brief and unspectacular career, this type was consigned to history. On one occasion I saw a formation of twelve and on others a few singles.

The Boulton-Paul Defiant, a single-engined two-seat fighter whose design philosophy was somewhat reminiscent of several World War One types, began its operational life over the beaches of Dunkirk at the time of the evacuation. Its initial success was due to all the armament being concentrated in a 4x.303 inch power operated gun turret mounted to fire aft and abeam behind the pilot. This type looked rather like a Hurricane in plan form and Luftwaffe pilots attacking from the rear and above in the normal manner often found their planes being shot to pieces before they realised their mistake. This of course was fine while it lasted, but as soon as the enemy got wise they adopted the obvious tactic of attacking from dead astern and below without the Defiant's gunner being able to fire a round! This spelt disaster and expediency dictated that being utterly outclassed in the role of day fighter, the survivors should only operate at night. They did; without distinction.

They were soon supplanted by the infinitely superior Beaufighter with its formidable armament of 4x20mm cannon and 6x.303 machine guns enhanced by its ability to "home in" on its victim with the new A.I (Air Interception) equipment.

One of the first raiders to be intercepted by this welcome innovation fell near Ringwood to the guns of "Cat's Eyes" Cunningham flying from Middle Wallop near Andover. Of all the inadvertant strokes of good fortune that befell anyone trying to prove a point this incident must rank very highly. On the evening in question, His Majesty King George the Sixth had been invited to see the new G.C.I. (Ground Controlled Interception) equipment in action at Sopley. Not only was he able to watch the contact made and the target handed over to the night fighter from within, he was able to step outside and witness the German raider plunging down in flames!

The name "Cat's Eyes" was a deliberate invention by the authorities to attribute super-normal eyesight to this pilot whose victories, so the propagandists told us, were the direct result of a diet consisting almost exclusively of carrots! Whether the enemy were fooled by this attempt to keep the secret of the little black box with the cathode ray tube I do not know, but we children were encouraged by our parents to eat plenty of carrots to enable us to cope with the blackout!

Another idea used to combat the night raiders was the Turbinlight. This was to all intents and purposes a searchlight mounted on a Havoc, the night fighter version of the Boston. The mode of operation was for the Havoc to illuminate the target which was then in theory destroyed by a Hurricane flying in consort. However, there were many imponderables concerned and to the best of my knowledge, despite the fact that several planes were so equipped for some two years, not one victory was recorded.

To return to the Defiant. Having been withdrawn from front-line service, those remaining were converted for target towing duties alongside the Lysanders which had been similarly relegated. Both types were a common sight locally with the yellow and black undersurface stripes denoting their function.

Despite the Lysander's obsolescence as an army co-operation type, it performed much useful service besides target towing. There was a constant requirement for "ditched" aircrew to be rescued and in co-operation with the Air Sea Rescue launches crewed by R.A.F. personnel the "Lizzies" were instrumental in saving the lives of many wet and exhausted flyers.

In addition, its short take-off and landing abilities enabled it to be used as an ideal ferry aircraft for secret agents moving in and out of enemy occupied Europe. These aircraft were painted matt black all over and one was still to be seen at Beaulieu aerodrome early in 1945. Nearby Exbury House (home of the famous Rothschild rhododendron and azalea gardens) was a training camp for agents during the war years and it seems more than probable that there was a connection.

The introduction of radio beams as a means of detecting aircraft was made by the British subsequent to the research and developement springing from its invention by Watson-Watt's team of "boffins" (scientists). The chain of "radiolocation" stations enabling Fighter Command to have advance warning of an impending attack by the enemy was one of the key factors in the Battle of Britain as was the A.I. in the battle against the night raiders. Many variations of the theme were developed, e.g. A.S.V. (Air to Surface Vessel) I.F.F. (Identification Friend or Foe) and so on and before long they were comprehensively known as Radar, a term originating in America and a derivative of Radio Detection and Ranging.

The basic idea of bouncing radio waves off an object, electrically analysing the resultant echo and displaying the "picture" on a calibrated screen was quite simple but there were many complications such as echoes of the wrong thing turning up and being misinterpreted. This "fly in the ointment" led to the idea of misleading the enemy who by the second year of the war had embarked on a crash programme to nullify the advantage enjoyed by the British in this field. Consequently, German radars were becoming not only sophisticated but effective.

In order to carry out this "spoofing" it was essential to obtain certain technical information and the only way in which this could be done was by capturing it from the enemy.

At Bruneval on the French coast near Le Harve stood a Wurtzburg main radar station and on a February night in 1942 a party of paratroops flying in a dozen Whitleys from Thruxton in northern Hampshire was dropped at the site together with an R.A.F. sergeant radar expert. The raid was one hundred per cent successful. The vital equipment was photographed, certain components purloined and the remainder of the installation blown up before the raiders retired to the beach to be picked up by the Royal Navy.

This brilliant exploit was the subject of a film made some years later, but its name unfortunately eludes me. In the film, the officer commanding the troops had been issued with instructions to shoot the sergeant if he was captured in order to prevent any secret information he had being tortured out of him, but whether this is the truth or a little dramatic licence I do not know.

The consequence of the Bruneval raid arrived one night over the New Milton and Highcliffe area. The sight that greeted us on looking out of the window the following morning was quite startling. Large numbers of metallic foil strips about the size of a school ruler littered the garden and hedges. The immediate reaction was to pick one up and examine it, but my father cautiously warned against it, thinking it could have been dropped by the Germans ("I mean, where else could it have come from?"). What it was no-one knew and speculation was rife, but one thing seemed certain; "Jerry" had dropped it and in some way not understood by anyone it was certain to be harmful. On arrival at school several of the lads had picked some up and they seemed to have come to no harm, but not even the teachers, who in our innocence we thought of as inexhaustable fountains of knowledge, were able to supply an explanation other than that it was something to do with the war!

In fact it was the first crude attempt at what today is termed E.C.M. (Electronic Counter Measures) and the culprits were not the Luftwaffe but almost certainly the Special Duties Flight by this time operating from Hurn and renamed the

Telecommunications Flying Unit. Crude or not, this experimental "jamming" paid off in a big way when used in "Operation Gomorrah", the proposed destruction of Hamburg by the R.A.F. which began seriously in July 1943. By that time almost all the enemy night fighters and anti-aircraft ("Flak") defences were radar controlled and the showers of foil (code name "Window") cluttered the screens with thousands of bogus "blips" depriving the enemy of his "eyes" with obvious advantages to the attackers.

The "cat and mouse" game which ensued with each side attempting to outwit the other in the radar battle is an intriguing story in its own right and was by no means a one-sided affair. One instance of how we came off second best was when I.F.F. was introduced on our bombers to detect enemy night fighters. (If any aircraft was not emitting the I.F.F. signal, it was assumed to be hostile.) As soon as they were able to discover the wavelength used by the R.A.F. they tuned in and were directed onto their targets by the very equipment intended for protection.

The Lockheed Hudson and North American Harvard were ordered in quantity by the British at an early stage of re-armament and both proved their worth. The Brewster Buffalo however was supplied only to our forces in the Far East and was an unmitigated disaster, the far superior Japanese fighters shooting them out of the Malayan skies with ease. The Boston proved a worthy successor to the Blenheim 4 and the Catalina and long range Liberators were doing sterling work in the battle against the U-boats whilst the Curtiss Tomahawks and Kittyhawks fought side by side with the Hurricanes and Desert Spitfires in North Africa.

One Liberator, serial number AL 504, had a particularly important assignment. It was the personal aircraft of Winston Churchill and was based at Hurn. Its name, "Commando" was highly appropriate, reflecting the war leader's tough and aggressive attitude towards the eventual victory of the Allied cause.

Despite the acquisition of all these aircraft from across the Atlantic more were needed desperately and the Allison engined P38 Lightning and P51 Mustang became available in 1942. The Lockheed Lightning was a "gift" for "spotters", but although this type operated from Ibsley during the latter half of 1942 I saw only the odd one or two. Its twin engine nacelles were elongated to become booms which supported the twin fins and rudders, whilst the pilot was accommodated in a single central pod. This design layout posed serious problems for the occupant in the event of having to leave the aircraft in flight and consequently the Lightning was considered to be a deathtrap. The only way it could be evacuated in an emergency with any hope of survival was to roll the aircraft on its back and literally fall out of it. I heard that this was successfully accomplished for the first time over Fordingbridge where the aircraft continued on to crash on a chicken farm.

Some Lightnings were obtained for the R.A.F.and those serving with the Americans went on to become one of the "big three" fighters, the others being the Republic P47 Thunderbolt and the Mustang from the North American stable.

The Mustang got off to a poor start. The evaluation flight (for the R.A.F.) was based at Hurn, but despite extravagant claims by the manufacturers, this type did not perform well at altitudes above about twelve thousand feet. Some were in fact taken onto the strength of the R.A.F., but only used by Army Co-operation Command in a low level tactical role. The problems they suffered were however overcome by re-engining with the Merlin, the well tried and highly successful British in-line used in such types as the Spitfire, Hurricane, Lancaster and Mosquito. There were insufficient Merlins available, but the problem was solved by allowing Packard to manufacture them under license in the U.S.A.. The resultant combination proved a happy marriage, particularly when the later marks of the Mustang were fitted with the "teardrop" cockpit covers providing all-round vision. These modifications together with refinements in the airframe design and increased tankage produced the finest long-range fighter of World War Two. The square-cut wings and tail unit gave this aeroplane a ruggedly pugnacious appearance well in keeping with its reputation as a deadly opponent in battle.

The "odd bods" of this period included a miniature Stirling. I thought I was seeing things as this tiny replica of the thirty-ton bomber passed overhead. It was not until after the war that I discovered that it was used to sort out some aerodynamic problems without going to the expense of using the real thing.

Another one-off was the Spitfire floatplane. Before Holmsley South became an operational aerodrome several areas of woodland had to be cleared at the runway approaches. My father was one of a gang employed at this task and as we were on school holidays I was helping. Imagine my delight when this most unusual Spitfire roared into view escorted by a squadron of normal Mark 5b's.

A further Spitfire variant was the Mark 11 with the duo-curves of its wings elongated to exaggerated points. This modification provided the extra wing area required to gain sufficient altitude to combat the Junkers 86r which had hitherto carried out its reconnaisance missions well above the height capable of being reached by any contemporary British fighter.

At that time one of the boys papers, "The Hotspur" I believe, carried a story of a plane with similar pointed wingtips sharpened like knives with which it tore into the enemy. This was usually in the split second before a stick of bombs was released onto a factory manufacturing "the secret weapon that would win the war"!

No such romantic adventures for the pilots of the real thing; more often a gruelling climb into the altitudes where the temperature plummeted to unheard of depths, a short patrol and not a glimpse of the enemy.

The requirement then was for a purpose built high altitude fighter. The Westland Welkin, successor to the Whirlwind and obviously based upon its design, but with very high aspect ratio wings, was the result, but by the time production was under way the need had evaporated. Although a substantial number were built none, as far as I know, ever fired a shot in anger.

Such was the nature of the war and like so many other projects, the rapidly changing pattern of events made this one obsolete at birth. Westland found little to contribute to the war effort from its design team. Their success was to come later when they became Britain's main manufacturer of helicopters.

In the early part of the war the magnetic mine was taking a tremendous toll of Allied (and neutral) shipping. A small number of Wellingtons were converted to carry a huge metal ring attached to the wings and fuselage, which powered by an on-board generator became a magnet. When flown over the sea at about fifty feet any mines in the vicinity were harmlessly exploded. Although somewhat hazardous, this method of dealing with what was indeed a deadly threat filled the gap until shipping was fitted with degaussing apparatus which neutralised the magnetic field of a vessel so equipped, thus rendering this type of undersea menace impotent.

I saw several of these planes (or more probably the same one several times). On browsing through my records I find that one was spotted as late as May 1945, perhaps indicating that they were being used at the end of the war to clear mines sown by the Allies.

One morning in, I think, 1942 I was awakened by a strange flapping noise. Looking out I could see nothing but fog which was stirring in a slight breeze. Utterly bewildered, in company with everyone else in the house, I went exploring with my father. All we could find was a cable attached to a telegraph pole in the field (which has since been developed as a timber and builders merchant's store (Jewsons). The pole was leaning at an angle and above it the cable disappeared into the mist from which the lazy flapping sound continued to emanate. It was pretty obvious that the cable belonged to a barrage balloon and later as the air became clear we were able to see it. It was unlike the rounded, rather dumpy type which we were used to, but elongated with smaller fins.

Purely by chance, Charlie Ballam was on leave from Balloon Command and staying with his sister further down Gore Road. We went and informed him and he made the necessary arrangements to have it removed. When this happened I was at school and missed seeing anything; I was most disappointed!

It transpired that our "visitor" was of a German design and having seemingly broken loose in a gale, had been blown across the Channel before its trailing mooring rope became entangled in the telegraph wires.

Long range Liberators based at Beaulieu were often seen on their journeys to and from the Bay of Biscay and beyond, where their presence was a considerable deterrant to the U-boats. Sometimes a contact would be made and depth charges dropped. Sometimes indeed a hit would be confirmed and on more than one occasion the attack took place from such a low altitude that the explosions damaged the aircraft which was then faced with the prospect of limping back to the nearest airfield, Predannack, on the Lizard peninsula. These attacks were few and far between with by far the greater part of the patrols spent quartering seemingly endless vistas of sea and sky.

A friend of mine, Don Turner, flew many Hudson sorties with 53 Squadron from St. Eval in Cornwall, but on only one occasion got a "blip" on the radar which indicated a U-boat. The aircraft dived to attack, dropped its depth charges on the swirl of foam created by the submerging submarine and as Don slid out the ventral machine gun to fire at the rapidly disappearing conning tower, a Catalina flying boat, approaching from the opposite direction came between him and his target! Luckily he did not fire. The U-boat was confirmed as damaged, the Catalina disappeared as suddenly as it arrived and the whole incident was over in a few hectic minutes. Half an hour's "stooging" in the area produced nothing further.

Life for the aircrew engaged on these vital activities was inevitably like this, but at all times a high state of alertness had to be maintained, not only with regard to ships but also Junkers 88's which all too often were ready to pounce upon the unwary.

The need for these patrols was so desperate in mid-1942 that student crews flying Whitleys from the O.T.U. (Operational Training Unit) at St. Eval were routed over the sea in an attempt, successful to a degree, to keep the U-boats submerged.

Whilst the Liberators operated from Beaulieu, a similar task was being undertaken by Wellingtons and Whitleys and at a later stage by Halifaxes from Holmsley South over nearer waters. As time passed the radar antennae systems used by these aircraft became more complicated and were clearly visible from the ground as were the ventral "blisters" housing the H2S apparatus.

I was always puzzled that the camouflage used on these aircraft, like that of the Sunderlands was predominantly white with some grey. They always stood out distinctly against a dark cloud background, particularly in strong sunlight; not, one would have thought, the best way of remaining hidden.

Holmsley South and Beaulieu, although geographically some nine miles apart, nevertheless shared a problem; the circuits used by their respective aircraft overlapped. This unfortunate circumstance was brought sharply into focus on 13th August 1943 when a Wellington from Beaulieu collided with a Halifax climbing away from Holmsley. The Halifax crashed at Flexford and the "Wimpey" a short distance away near Hordle, killing all the members of both crews and in addition one unfortunate civilian. It is certainly surprising that this type of accident was not more frequent when one considers the incredibly large numbers of aircraft in the air at any one time in those desperate days.

One of the very few Catalinas I saw during the course of the war showed itself at about a thousand feet one afternoon through the only gap in a sky full of low cloud; like the flaming Junkers 88, a two-second exposure on the photographic film of my memory.

Another maritime type was the Walrus amphibian that occasionally passed our way. Directly descended from the Schneider Trophy designs of the 1920's (which eventually never competed) and originally designated Seagull Mark *5*, anything less like a racing aircraft would he difficult to imagine. With its pusher engine mounted between the wings, which were situated above the hull, it looked extremely archaic.

Nevertheless it did excellent service in the search and rescue role and like the Lysander mentioned earlier was responsible for many aircrew, some 7,000 in all, living to fly another day. The advantage enjoyed by the Walrus over the "Lizzie" was its ability to alight on the water in anything up to a sea producing five foot waves.

Some of these Walruses were based at Sandbanks at the entrance to Poole Harbour and operated in conjunction with the Air Sea Rescue launches at Hamworthy. This must have been one of the most sought after postings in the British Isles. Not only was it in an extremely pleasant geographical location, it was near Bournemouth; and perhaps best of all, the Officers Mess was situated at the Harbour Heights Hotel, one of the most luxurious in an area where luxury was taken for granted, even in those austere times.

Incidentally its nickname was the "Shagbat" which seemed singularly appropriate. For the benefit of those not well versed in RAF. legend I should explain that the Shagbat was a mythical Egyptian bird whose habit it was to fly round in ever-decreasing circles until it disappeared up its own fundamental orifice!

The C.G. 13a and the CC. 4a were two American gliders sometimes seen being towed by Dakotas, probably from Stoney Cross in the northern New Forest. The standard British training type, the Hotspur, put in the odd appearance behind a Martinet and occasionally a Hamilcar, the Tetrarch tank carrier, lumbered across my vision in the wake of a Halifax, the only aircraft capable of pulling it.

I have often regretted not keeping some sort of record of the middle years of the war as at one time or another I must have seen almost every type that was in service in that period. In addition to those previously mentioned I have recollections of the following which spring immediately to mind:- Crane (the British version of the Cessna Bobcat and the approximate equivalent of the Oxford), Hudson, Argus, Beaufort, Stirling, Firefly, Piper Cub, Avenger, Lancaster, Norseman, Martlet (later marks were named Wildcat in conformity with the American version.), Typhoon, Fulmar, Auster, Beaufighter, Boston, Sentinel, Blenheim, Swordfish, Mosquito, Mitchell, Fortress, Anson. etc. It is my guess that had I in fact recorded every type I saw at that time over one hundred names would have been on my list.

Spitfires and Hurricanes, still the backbone of a rapidly expanding Fighter Command, were always to be seen. New developments of the original designs were often in evidence, particularly the Spitfire, to me the epitome of British aeronautical engineering excellence.

A few years ago, one of my daughters gave me a picture of one, which now hangs in the lounge of my home. I often pause to admire its almost magical lines which never pall. It is a matter of record that this incredible aircraft stayed in continuous production from March 1936 until October '47. In all, well over twenty thousand in twenty-four marks were manufactured in addition to Seafires and even then the design potential was not exhausted. The Spiteful (and the navalised Seafang), albeit with an entirely re-designed "laminar flow" wing, still owed much to its progenitor!

A further indication of its development lies in the fact that the Griffon 65 developed 2,375hp. to drive a contra-rotating propeller in the latest marks as compared with the original Merlin with its I,050hp and the two-bladed fixed pitch wooden "prop" of the Mark 1.

The U.S. Eighth Air Force had started arriving in Britain early in 1942 as part of its build-up for the daylight onslaught against Hitler's Europe, which commenced on 17th August.

My first sighting of a Flying Fortress took place on a Sunday afternoon whilst cycling between Bransgore and Ringwood. I can remember the exact spot and I am often reminded of that day when I pass it. From that time on the big silver bombers became a regular sight.

Although the standard function of the Fortress was that of a conventional bomber, some were used as reconnaissance aircraft and others as transports, air-sea rescue lifeboat carriers, target drones, gun-ship formation protectors and the like.

One little known use to which some were put was as Aphrodite guided missiles. These unmanned aircraft were packed with some six tons of high explosive and targeted onto U-boat pens on the French Atlantic coast and although I have never heard what results were attained it seems unlikely that they had much success. One can imagine that the power of penetration achieved against sixteen feet of reinforced concrete was virtually nil; certainly nowhere near that of the specially designed "Earthquake Bomb" used by the Lancasters of 617 Squadron.

Enemy activity over this period was spasmodic. No longer did we listen in trepidation as we had on the nights when waves of bombers passed over the German radio beam which crossed the English coast at Hengistbury Head. No longer were we awakened by the siren nearly every night, but nevertheless there were still occasions when "Jerry" made his presence known; and felt !

One night I was lying under the table shelter my father had built in the living room and under which we now slept as a matter of course. The unmistakable throbbing of German aero-engines gradually increased in volume and then there were six heavy explosions each louder than its predecessor and each preceded by a whistle.

I waited in fearful anticipation, expecting the next one to blow us all to smithereens whilst the door and windows were rattled furiously as if by an unseen hand.

As it turned out the nearest bomb to us landed nearly a mile away, but there was one whistle without a bang and this could mean but one thing; an unexploded bomb! It was discovered in the garden of "Golden Acre", a bungalow behind the "Walkford Hotel".

The Bomb Disposal Squad was soon on the scene but alarm and despondency set in among the "regulars" when they heard that the bomb had come to rest in a seam of shifting sand several feet down and was slowly but surely making its way towards the cellar of the hotel. Happily, the bomb was exploded underground at the third attempt without too much damage and every drinker sighed with relief!

What was reputed to be an airborne torpedo dropped on Chewton Common, between Highcliffe and Walkford leaving a huge crater almost twenty feet deep. The siren had not sounded and I was having my "weekly" in the tin bath in front of the fire. At the terrific bang, I dived for cover under the shelter upsetting the bath in the process!

Luckily there was only superficial damage to property from the explosion and no-one was hurt. The crater soon filled naturally and served as a static water source for the NFS (National Fire Service) until it was reinstated and used as a baseball pitch by the "Yanks" when they were encamped there prior to D-day. Even now its outline can still be traced beneath the fern.

New Milton suffered two more attacks in this period. One Saturday afternoon I saw a Heinkel 111 "cloud hopping" at about 500ft above Christchurch. It was memorable because I had seen it so closely, but it became more so when it was learnt that it had deposited its load on the Spencer Road area where some of the bombs had fallen in August 1940. Deaths and injuries were again caused, but by comparison with the previous attack it was fairly minor.

The other occasion was on the evening of 22 January, 1943. I had visited the "Waverley" cinema at New Milton (opposite Barton Court Road) and walked home. When I arrived I was astonished at being greeted with considerable relief. I had heard a German aircraft overhead, but by that period of the war nobody took much notice of engines in the night. Imagine my surprise when I learned that a house in Vincent Road had received a direct hit and all its occupants, Mrs. Morin and her three small daughters, killed. I could have not been more than a quarter of a mile away and heard nothing. My parents, a quarter of a mile further on again, most certainly bad!

In July 1943 I left school and started work and in the autumn joined the Ashley Flight, 1308 Squadron, Air Training Corps. My ambition was steadily becoming a real possibility. I looked forward eagerly to each issue of "The Aeroplane Spotter" and continued to become even more absorbed in the world of aircraft.

Four of my older friends were by this time in the R.A.F.. Len Morris was a Halifax gunner, Tony Hardy was piloting Lancasters, Fred Kettle was an engine fitter and Jack Hall an "Ack Ack" gunner with the R.A.F. Regiment at "Hellfire Corner" on the Kent coast.

I was present one day when Len and Jack were both on leave and chatting about matters of mutual interest. "Have you got a motto with your lot?", asked Jack. "Yes", replied Len with obvious pride, "Press on regardless." "We've got one too", said Jack, "Like the L.D.V., Look, duck and vanish!" Len won the Distinguished Flying Medal and rose to be a warrant officer, and Jack cheerfully remained an "A.C. Plonk".

Another airman was Mr. Brooks, the teacher who foretold the result of the Battle of Britain. He, poor chap, had joined the meteorological branch of the R.A.F. and spent most of his service far away in the virtual isolation of the Shetland Isles (or was it the Orkneys?) He and I corresponded regularly until he was demobilised at around the time that I joined up and in the way that things sometimes work out we never met again although he resumed his teaching career at Ashley. I saw his obituary in the local newspaper a few years ago and sadly wondered why.

One sometimes tends to forget that when air-crew are carrying out their duties, they are still prey to the normal aches and pains of everyday life; perhaps even more so with the stress factor inherent in their task. Such was the situation in which Tony Hardy found himself whilst engaged on a diversionary mission over the Channel Islands. A slight pain in his abdomen had developed rapidly into appendicitis. In severe pain, he carried out his mission and collapsed as he stepped down from the Lancaster on his arrival back at base.

I have often pondered which action is the more deserving of a medal, one such as this or a spontaneous reaction to circumstance accompanied by a little luck? Of one thing I have no doubt. The courage of lads, many too young to be officially classed as men, who time after time ventured cheerfully into the hostile night skies of Europe was second to none. To be willingly subjected to the most terrifying ordeal of flying straight and level on the bombing run in the face of everything the enemy could throw at them was bad enough. In addition to this, the "normal" hazards of wartime flying and the prospect of no more seeing comrades who had "bought it" were poor companions on the long, boring journey back across the North Sea with the prospect of a fog diversion just for good measure. These men were truly heroes and I longed to be one of them.

CHAPTER 4
A TIME APART.

1944 was a year when I lived more intensely than I had ever lived before, but it is only in retrospect that I am able to really recognise the fact.

My work had to do with the manufacture of components for Bristol Hercules aero-engines for such types as the Beaufighter, Halifax, Wellingon, Stirling,etc.. A poster on the wall of the New Milton Sheet Metal Works in Old Milton Road, the factory where I learned what real work was, included a Sunderland among the types using this particular engine. Enthusiastic the artist may have been, but he (or she) was also ignorant of the fact that the Sunderland used Pegasus engines with the exception of the Mark 5 which was powered by the American Pratt and Whitney "Twin Wasp". However, this poster did its job; it provided a focus for the repetitive and boring mass production work. It was good to know that standing at a parting-off machine, repeating the same series of opertions sixteen hundred times a day and becoming soaked with slurry really had the significance that had it not been done, hundreds of aircraft would never have flown. To look into the sky and see a "Halibag" for example and to know that there was a good chance that it carried my small contribution gave me a real feeling of pride. Then the aching arms and blistered hands seemed a very small sacrifice!

Food production was a high priority in wartime and consequently we kept dozens of rabbits and chickens and in addition cultivated a large vegetable garden and allotment. Together with my work which sometimes included unofficial overtime for which I was slipped the odd ten bob (50p) note, there was not too much time for other activities, but I still managed to attend all the A.T.C. meetings and journey round on my cycle, visiting the local airfields.

On my travels, usually in company with a friend or two, I was also able to observe and marvel at the phenomenal build-up of war material destined for the "Second Front". The whole of the New Forest area was rapidly becoming a giant munitions complex with tanks, guns, lorries and all manner of lesser vehicles parked everywhere. Roads had been strengthened and country lanes widened to accommodate the logistic requirements of this incredible enterprise. Dumps of food, ammunition and all manner of military stores sheeted down with camouflaged tarpaulins or netting seemed to fill almost every piece of spare ground and there were thousands upon thousands of troops of many nationalities mostly living under canvas or in their vehicles. All this was of course in addition to the airfields and the Ashley bombing range at Godshill to the north. This was the range where, besides testing the 4,000lb "Blockbuster", the 22,000lb "Grand Slam" and Barnes Wallis's bouncing bomb, many captured enemy vehicles were attacked to determine the effectiveness of Allied bombs and rocket projectiles.

In a roadside copse between Bransgore and Ringwood a field hospital had been set up by the Americans and one Sunday afternoon Lou Collins, an A.T.C. friend, and myself helped unload a three ton truck laden with wooden boxes marked "SILVERTEX PROPHYLACTICS. FOR THE USE OF U.S. ARMY PERSONNEL ONLY". Upon inquiry we were told that the contents with the strange name which neither of us had ever heard before were "French Letters" (condoms). It seemed certain that there would soon be plenty of action in Normandy whether or not there was any fighting! I think we were agreed that if the "Yanks" were as good at fighting as they appeared to be at certain other activities, then we did not have much to worry about!

On another occasion at the same camp we were amazed to see a patient being operated on in a theatre tent with the side walls rolled up (presumably because of the heat). This meant that it was virtually in the open air, but in practical terms it was probably a luxury that would not always be afforded in the days to come. It was clearly in view from the public road only a few yards away, but it was an established fact that the American idea of security was the odd G.I. wandering around with a rifle and little else.

Sometimes now when driving through the Forest, deserted apart from a few cattle and ponies and possibly the odd rider, my mind travels back to those stirring times and I can picture again the scene as it was then and wonder if it really happened; but happen it did!

During 1943, both Hurn and Holmsley South were host to Transport Command operating Stirlings and Halifaxes in the Airborne Support role mainly towing Horsas. Many of the Horsas taking part in the debacle of the airborne assault on Sicily ("Operation Beggar") which achieved little apart from the knowledge of what not to do, started their journey to North Africa from here. The first leg of the trip was to Portreath in Cornwall, the nearest British airfield to their destination, Morocco. The thirteen hundred intervening miles meant a flight time of something like ten hours. The first part of this journey, over the Bay of Biscay, could be extremely hazardous because of its proximity to enemy territory and a Halifax with its bomb bays loaded with petrol tanks to achieve the necessary range and unable to take anything other than mild evasive action without casting loose its glider, was a sitting target for prowling Ju 88's.

But there were perils distinct from the inherent risks involved in the strangely code-named "Turkey Buzzard" hauls in preparation for "Beggar". On 16th May (1943) a Holmsley Halifax crashed with an engine fire on its way to pick up a Horsa from Hurn. Disaster struck suddenly at the most critical point of take-off and without sufficient power the aircraft plunged to its destruction on a piece of waste ground off Thatchers Lane in Bransgore. There were no survivors.

One British and two Canadian crew members now lie in the peace of the airmen's corner at Bransgore churchyard where the birds still sing and the buttercups and purple orchis decorate the graves in May as they did in that May of half a century ago. I stood there in silence and paid my tribute on the 50th anniversary of the day those young men died in a war that gave us the peace we have enjoyed ever since.

Their sacrifice was no less than that of those who died in battle and we owe them our homage.

One frosty morning in the following February I was helping a friend, Jack Coombes, repair a roof in New Milton when away in the West a great growling roar began to fill the air. The sun was brilliant and then above the trees we saw it glinting on the shapes of aircraft. The noise became thunderous as the tugs and gliders sailed majestically through the otherwise still air; wave upon wave they came until it seemed that they almost covered the entire sky. Gradually the volume of sound abated and then Jack turned to me and said, "Caw, bugger me!" I find it difficult to imagine a more appropriate comment. I believe this gigantic demonstration of airborne might was "Exercise Mallard", a rehearsal for the real thing which was soon to take place over Normandy.

Shortly after this, Transport Command withdrew to bases further inland to enable the airfields nearest France to be used by the fighter-bombers in the softening up process which was the prerequisite of the invasion. So T.A.F. (Tactical Airfield) 83 arrived. These "Tactical Airfields" were self-contained units capable of moving from place to place as the war situation demanded.

Instead of Hercules engines with their throaty roar, the whine of Merlins and the somewhat heavier note of the Napier Sabres now provided the background music to the great epic being enacted around us. Hurricanes, Typhoons, Spitfires and Mosquitos formed the equipment, each contributing in its own way to the destruction of the French rail network and transport system besides many other targets.

At Hurn, 500 and 1,000lb bombs and 60lb rocket projectiles were stacked beneath camouflage nets a few yards from the public highway. They, in addition to its standard armament of 4x2Omm cannon, provided the "punch" for the Typhoon with its huge air intake beneath the equally huge propeller needed to absorb the 2,000h.p. produced by the Sabre engine. Incidentally, the ground clearance of the propeller was only seven inches when the fuselage was level and considerable skill was required during take-off and landing to avoid ploughing up the runway!

Soon after this time when their primary targets had been the enemy radar installations, the Typhoon earned the nickname of "The Flying Tin-opener". How appropriate this was! It was certainly well testified to by the large number of disabled enemy armoured vehicles which littered the killing grounds of Mortaine and the Fallaise Pocket. From an unpromising start as a fighter plagued by technical problems and at one time on the point of abandonment, this aircraft emerged as the scourge of the Panzers and without doubt contributed vastly to the success of Allied arms in the later stages of the war in Europe.

Besides what have since come to be known as strike aircraft, Mark 16 Mosquito night fighters flew interdiction sorties from both Hurn and Holmsley, often catching German planes as they were landing. Their daylight counterparts ranged far and wide over the Continent, searching out "targets of opportunity" and hammering them with bombs, cannon, rockets and machine-guns.

At Holmsley one evening, a Mosquito returning from the last sortie of the day was preparing to land as I watched from the nearby A35. It was using the runway which ran parallel to the road and approached from the East in the normal manner. As the wheels touched down it abruptly upended itself thrusting its nose into the tarmac. It was too far away to see the result in detail, but the fire tender and the "blood wagon" were immediately on the scene.

Strangely enough I witnessed an almost identical accident at Pershore in 1947 when a Mosquito landed with the wheel brakes still on. That incident cost both of the crew their lives and I was a member of the burial party for the pilot, a New Zealander.

Holmsley's station "hack" in the D-Day period was a Harvard. Built by North American, this low-wing, two-seal trainer had the unquestioned reputation of being the noisiest plane in the air. With the propeller set in coarse pitch the resultant rasping note was guaranteed to put anyone's teeth on edge as it assaulted the eardrums! Despite this disadvantage, the "Yellow Peril" as it was affectionately known, did sterling work throughout the war and well beyond. In fact there are still several airworthy examples which have survived the intervening years and although the noise element has failed to mellow, it still tingles the spine with a nostalgic thrill.

At Somerford, Horsas continued to come off the production line, now in the Mark 2 version with a single towing point above the twin nose wheels. This was a considerable advance on the bifurcated rope and proved much easier to handle by the ground crews. Another advantage was that it enabled a cable angle indicator ("angle-dangle" in the vernacular) to be used, thus assisting the glider pilot in determining his position relative to the towing aircraft in cloud.

In addition to the Horsas, Spitfires were being modified to Seafire standards to allow them to operate from aircraft carriers. This called for the addition of an arrester hook and other ancillary items. I heard at one time that some were fitted with RATOG (Rocket Assisted Take-off Gear) but have never seen any evidence of this.

The Fleet Air Arm, in the form of H.M.S. Raven, was also using the airfield to install and upgrade their airborne radar systems. Consequently there was much coming and going by a large selection of types which included the Fulmar, Avenger, Reliant, Firefly, Swordfish, Blenheim 4, Martlet and Barracuda.

One most unlikely Royal Navy visitor at a later date was a Stirling! I was intrigued that such a massive aircraft should be on the strength of the F.A.A. but soon found that it was used to ferry crewmen and equipment, obviously a much quicker method of transport than the traditional one. "Massive" was certainly the right adjective to apply to this converted bomber which was once described as "an aircraft designed solely to lift its undercarriage off the ground!"

In March the U.S. Ninth Air Force also arrived at Somerford. A new mesh and perforated metal runway had previously been constructed on the eastern side of the airfield between Humphrey's Bridge and Mudeford to accommodate the Thunderbolts, or as they were known to their pilots, "Thunderbabies" of 405 Fighter Group. Two more similar landing strips, rudimentary in the extreme, had also been laid down at Bisterne and Winkton for the same type of aircraft. That at Bisteme suffered from poor consolidation of the soil and was in fact unusable for much of its intended life.

The Thunderbolt, a single seat fighter/dive bomber was produced by the Republic Aircraft Corporation as a successor to the Lancer to which it bore a superficial resemblance although its performance and warload were much superior. It was easily recognised by its rather tubby appearance, large radial engine and wings with a plan form reminiscent of the Spitfire. Before they arrived locally I had never seen one, but for the next three months or so, despite all the other planes coming and going, Thunderbolts dominated the scene.

Although the pilots were told by General Eisenhower, the Supreme Allied Commander that they would be worked as airmen had never been worked before, they achieved little fame. Their job was the unspectacular attrition of the German defences in France prior to and during the Invasion and as such was gallantly fulfilled. Day after day if the weather permitted these intrepid young men would take to the air sometimes as many as three, four or even more times a day often relying on benzidrene tablets ("Blue Bennies") to keep them awake.

This intensity of operations was however not confined to the Americans and it is interesting to note that at Needs Oar Point, a temporary airfield situated near the mouth of the Beaulieu River and operating 150 Typhoons, some 900 sorties were flown in one day! This official figure signifies a sustained rate of one take-off every minute or so plus an appropriate number of landings, sadly somewhat fewer. It also follows that at least six sorties were flown by every aircraft! Neither should it be forgotten that in this period of extended maximum effort this was not an isolated instance.

An intriguing incident occurred at this location on 18th April `44. A Junkers 188 had arrived overhead and was flying in an apparently nonchalant manner above the vast military concentrations. Needless to say, this action provoked an immediate response and the intruder was quickly shot down by a flight of Typhoons. On the face of it, an extremely cheeky attempt to obtain valuable photographic evidence of the Allied forces in the area had been foiled.

Examining this incident in more detail, it transpires that the `188 took no avoiding action; neither did it fire its guns. Moreover, it discharged a series of red star shells, a recognised distress signal. Perhaps considered in a more leisurely manner than appears to have been the case, these gestures may have been construed as communicating the same message that a white flag would signify on the battlefield.

As far as I am aware, no conclusive proof of this theory has emerged; neither has it been discounted, but the fact that there were more dead bodies in the wreckage than the normal crew (four or five), would seem to indicate that in all probability, the aircraft had been "hijacked" and intended landing at Beaulieu in the same way that a German training type had landed at Somerford earlier in the war.

There is an interesting sequal to this wartime mystery. Neville Shute, the author and founder of the Airspeed company, tells of an imaginary, but very similar incident in his novel, "Requiem for a Wren" first published in 1955. The geographical location is identical, as is the period, the main difference being that the aircraft is destroyed by fire from the ground.

One can imagine that Mr. Shute was well aware of what had occurred and was sufficiently impressed for it to become the core around which his superb story was written.

But to return to the Thunderbolts. On occasions their duties would be varied by a medium range bomber escort mission, for which they used compressed cardboard auxiliary fuel tanks carried beneath the wings and fuselage. Many of these were converted into extremely unsafe canoes by the local lads after they had been left behind when the Americans departed.

The servicing of these aircraft was carried out on a typically American mass-production basis, specific areas of responsibility being allocated to specialist groundcrew within a certain trade. Unlike the R.A.F. system where for example a rigger would be trained in every aspect of airframe maintenance, the Americans were trained in only one small area; so they became "mainplane men", "landing gear men", etc.

Between the location of the Winkton airstrip and the "Lamb Inn" there still exists a wide ancient lane. In those action packed days of 1944, that "time apart", when the whole character of Southern Hampshire utterly changed, this area was the bomb dump. Bombs would arrive by rail at Christchurch and be collected in the large "cattle truck" lorries much used by the gum-chewing "Yanks". On arrival at the dump, complete with "rolling rings" but without tailfins, they would be literally thrown off the trucks, much to our amazement. Of course they were minus the fuses so what at first sight appeared to be a potentially suicidal method of handling was in fact quite safe. There never seemed to be anything more than a roll of barbed wire between thousands of tons of high explosive and the general public, but with the usual laxity of our allies, mentioned before, that was the way things were.

In addition to Winkton, Bisterne and Somerford there was another Thunderbolt airstrip at Snooks Farm, Pylewell (Lymington) and they also operated from the properly developed aerodromes at Beaulieu, and Ibsley. From these "hornets nests" they would climb into formation before "going over", the Pratt and Whitney "Double Wasp" engines labouring under a full load of fuel and "stores" which brought the all-up weight to almost seven tons. (An interesting comparison puts an equally loaded Hurricane at a little over half this weight!)

On one unforgetable occasion, we counted around two hundred of them in one great cloud. Another time, the A.T.C. were on church parade at St. Thomas's, Lymington. During the service a string of returning Thunderbolts began landing at Pylewell and the din of their engines was so great that the proceedings had to be abandoned until they were all down.

Because of the constant strain and pressure to which the pilots, groundcrews and aircraft were subjected, accidents did occur. Two of these were really serious. On one occasion two fully bombed-up Thunderbolts were taking off but had failed to observe the rules regarding the distance between aircraft. The consequence was that they collided with an almighty explosion at the Mudeford end of the Somerford runway, catching another plane in the blast and causing extensive damage to the nearby bungalows and several casualties, some fatal. The other incident involved a bungalow in Lingwood Avenue upon which another Thunderbolt, again fully laden with fuel and bombs and piloted by a surviving pilot of the previous accident once more crashed on take-off. The resulting casualties included nineteen deaths. It must be said that the foregoing details of these crashes are related as I understand them to have occurred, but other accounts differ slightly.

The weight of these aircraft continually rolling over the Sommerfield mesh runway did not improve the surface and on several occasions bombs were inadvertently shed during take-off, luckily without mishap.

Often in the evenings, I would cycle down to Somerford to see what was happening. One Sunday, in company with Phil Breaker, my companion when we saw the Ju88 which bombed New Milton, I was at Humphrey's Bridge watching the Thunderbolts landing. The "Snowdrops", American military police so called because of the white helmets they wore, always halted the traffic in Highcliffe Road when aircraft were landing as the flight path lay directly overhead. We were chatting to them as we often did, partly because we sometimes "clicked" for some cigarettes. (The "Yanks" were normally very liberal in this respect and to us, the "Lucky Strike", "Camel", "Old Gold, "Raleigh", "Chesterfield" and the other soft-packed brands were quite exotic.)

During the "stream" landing, a coloured soldier came pedalling across the grass towards us wobbling unsteadily on his cycle, as he pointed excitedly into the air. A returning plane was circling at about 3,000 ft and as we stared upwards one of the wings, almost detached from the fuselage was slowly but visibly flapping. We stared, fascinated. The soldier told us that the pilot was turning the plane out to sea and "jumping" and sure enough, almost as he spoke, a figure fell from the stricken fighter and a white parachute billowed out above him. The plane was unfortunately turned back inland by the typically stiff sea breeze of an April evening and crashed in the school playground at Highcliffe, whilst its former occupant descended unhurt in the recreation ground opposite.

The crash did not produce a fire and incredibly the only damage was one broken window, although clods of earth had been thrown everywhere and the fir trees opposite were festooned with sheets of aluminium cladding ripped from the wings and fuselage. Within a short time a Jeep bad whisked the pilot back to base where he soon became airborne again. This was a standard proceedure for pilots who had survived a crash in order to avoid them losing their nerve. The universal and heartfelt verdict on this incident was "Thank God the children were not in school at the time!".

On the Saturday before D-Day we watched all the planes being painted with "Invasion Stripes", black and white bands across fuselage and wings, hopefully enabling "trigger-happy" gunners to identify them as "Allied". All the aircraft involved in this colossal undertaking bore these distinctive markings, but unfortunately and perhaps inevitably, they did not always have the desired effect.

At the end of June when suitable airstrips became available in Normandy the Thunderbolts departed, leaving behind my indelible memories of a band of dedicated young warriors, no less courageous than "The Few", but alas, now equally as forgotten as "The Few" are remembered. A few Thunderbolts still used Somerford for a time and one of these had the unfortunate experience of landing short, skidding across Highcliffe Road and coming to rest just inside the airfield boundary; inverted!

The reconnaisance aircraft used in conjunction with the Thunderbolts was a Mustang, always parked alone near "Bure Homage" (requisitioned as officers` quarters, whilst the around crews slept under canvas and serviced their charges in the open). Its pilot was regarded as something of a daredevil and reputedly never flew without a hipflask of whiskey!

At Winkton in the same period, an R.A.F. Auster light observation plane was parked in an out-of-the-way corner of the airfield near the "Lamb Inn". Across the road, a radar post had been set up with three lorries, several conventional aerials and a "dish" aerial. We were told that this equipment was highly secret but heard later that the Auster was used for calibration purposes. This embryonic unit together with the G.C.I. station nearer Ripley eventually developed into the H.Q. of Southern Radar in the cold war expansion of the Fifties which operated through into the Seventies. As for the Auster, the last we saw of it was a cow with its horns (long before the clays of de-horning) hopelessly entangled in the wing fabric and tearing it to shreds!

Sometimes large formations of Fortresses up to almost one hundred strong passed overhead on their way to French targets from their bases in East Anglia. By the time they had reached our area, their height was sufficient to leave "contrails" in suitable weather conditions, a superb sight in the morning sun; but no doubt a terrifying one for those on the receiving end of their attentions. It was the custom to count them on the way out and again on their return and say a silent prayer for the others.

How I longed to be up there with them. I just could not wait; but I was only fifteen. Would the war last long enough for me to get in on the act? It was beginning to look unlikely. Could the enemy withstand the immense military might, a tiny part of which was so evident around me, in addition to the now unstoppable force of the Russians, by this time thrusting back towards the Third Reich? I was forced to admit that my youthful ambitions looked like remaining a dream (and as I have since come to realise, a romantic one).

On the 5th June I looked out from the Highcliffe cliffs and the sea off the Isle of Wight seemed crowded with ships, some with barrage balloons aloft. I knew then that what the whole country, indeed the whole free world had waited for so long was about to take place. Early next morning, before it was properly light I was awoken by a grumbling roar like distant thunder. Hundreds of heavy calibre naval guns opened up as the bombardment heralding "Operation Overlord" started and "Dunkirk" was being avenged. We were going back!

CHAPTER 5
MODIFIED AMBITIONS.

What had been a period of almost frenzied activity in the D-Day build-up soon evolved into a much quieter situation in every respect. Winkton, Bisteme and Pylewell had all served their purpose and lay abandoned. Likewise the Eastern part of Somerford, although of course the new runway was still used by its permanent residents. T.A.F.83 were not long in moving into liberated France leaving Hurn and Holmsley South suddenly almost deserted; but not for long!

An American hospital had been rapidly constructed at St. Leonard`s to accommodate casualties from the fighting in France and its proximity to Hurn enabled wounded soldiers to be air lifted in by Dakota with a minimum of delay. By comparison to the number of aircraft on strength at Hurn on D-Day, over two hundred Typhoons and Mosquitos, the Dakota flights were a mere dribble.

Then the medium bomber element of the Ninth Air Force arrived equipped with B26 Marauders, following T.A.F. 83 as they did at Holmsley South and also arriving at Beaulieu at about the same time in late July. These were tough twin-engined bombers intended for medium level bombing. Although successful in this role with a two ton load, some were modified for ground attack by the addition of detachable packages of .5 inch machine guns strapped to the fuselage and set to fire forward and down, bringing the total number of guns carried to fourteen! These were particularly effective against troop concentrations or columns of vehicles, the technique being to bomb at low level, turn through 180 degrees and strafe on the return.

The Marauder was unfortunately not the easiest of aircraft to handle and accidents were quite frequent with inexperienced pilots although as far as I am aware, no crashes occurred locally in the month or so that they were here. However, they were apparently detested by their crews and from the stories that we heard, their nickname, Widow Makers, was richly deserved.

The domestic site at Holmsley was situated in the wooded area between Harrow Farm and Forest Lodge with the W.A.A.F. site, "Out of bounds to all airmen", (at least officially) in a separate piece of copse.

At the entrance to the main site where the cinema and mess halls were situated stood a notice outside the guard room which read :- "ROYAL AIR FORCE, HOLMSLEY SOUTH." One of our allies had crudely painted out the "ROYAL" and substituted "YANKEE". We were quite offended by this lack of respect but had to admit that in effect what it said was true. However, of all the instances I have come across that illustrate the difference between the R.A.F. and the U.S.A.A.F. this is the one that says it all!

About this time I changed my employment and became a laboratory assistant at the Signals Research and Development Establishment (S.R.D.E. or still the "Hush

Hush') at Steamer Point close to Somerford Aerodrome. I was able to observe much of what went on there and although the Thunderbolts had left, the Fleet Air Aim was still very active on the original airfield. Airspeeds were as always going strong, and an Anson was much in use by S.R.D.E. for airborne trials of the highly secret equipment being developed. At that time George Errington who had distinguished himself some years earlier by flying an Airspeed Envoy into China, was Airspeed's chief test pilot and his personal Hornet Moth was often around. I believe it was at this time that the tug aircraft used for the Horsas was changed from a Whitley to a Halifax.

On 8th August I decided to keep a daily record of all the different types of aircraft I saw. I had on many occasions jotted down notes of various types seen, but this was to be an ongoing task. How I wish I had started it a few years earlier! My first book deals with the period up to the 27th of April 1945 and the first day's "bag" consisted of the following types: Liberator, Fortress, Whitley, Horsa, Crane, Thunderbolt, Oxford, Anson, Defiant, Piper Cub, Argus, Sentinel, Marauder, Dakota, Ventura, Lightning, Tiger Moth, Sunderland, Spitfire, Mustang. These twenty types are a fair representation of those planes around at that time. Browsing back over the record, several types are seen almost every day for a time and then their place is taken by others, thus reflecting the situation at any given time. What had started out as a youthful hobby developed into a historical document that may well be unique and which was used as the basis for a local history project by some of the pupils at Arnewood School, New Milton, under Arthur Lloyd, the local historian. At any event, it does provide a fascinating and nostalgic glimpse into the events of half a century ago. This book also contains a record of my flying log for the period (reproduced elsewhere in "Lure of the Blue.)

By this period of the war several Luftwaffe types had been captured by the Allies and formed into a "flying circus", Flight 1426, enabling our troops to actually see what these planes looked like in the air, as distinct from models and illustrations which had hitherto been the only source of information (unless of course they had seen the real thing!) This collection of "Jerries" had been used extensively prior to the invasion and I had half seen it once through the trees of the old Marley Avenue copse, which is now a bungalow estate. One type which it did not include was the Messerschmitt 410, but this type appears under the name Moskito on several occasions from mid-August, seeming to indicate that it was under test, possibly at Boscombe Down, the Air and Armaments Experimental Establishment on Salisbury Plain.

Incidentally, at that time my duties at work included the testing and evaluation of captured German radio components that as I recall compared very well with similar Allied equipment. This type of work was a far more leisurely process than the mass production to which I had grown accustomed and did in fact allow me time to pop out of the lab if I heard an aero-engine overhead. On reflection, this may well be the reason I started to keep my log.

One of the pieces of test equipment I used was a Wien Bridge which measured the capacitance of condensers. I soon found that by substituting a home-made

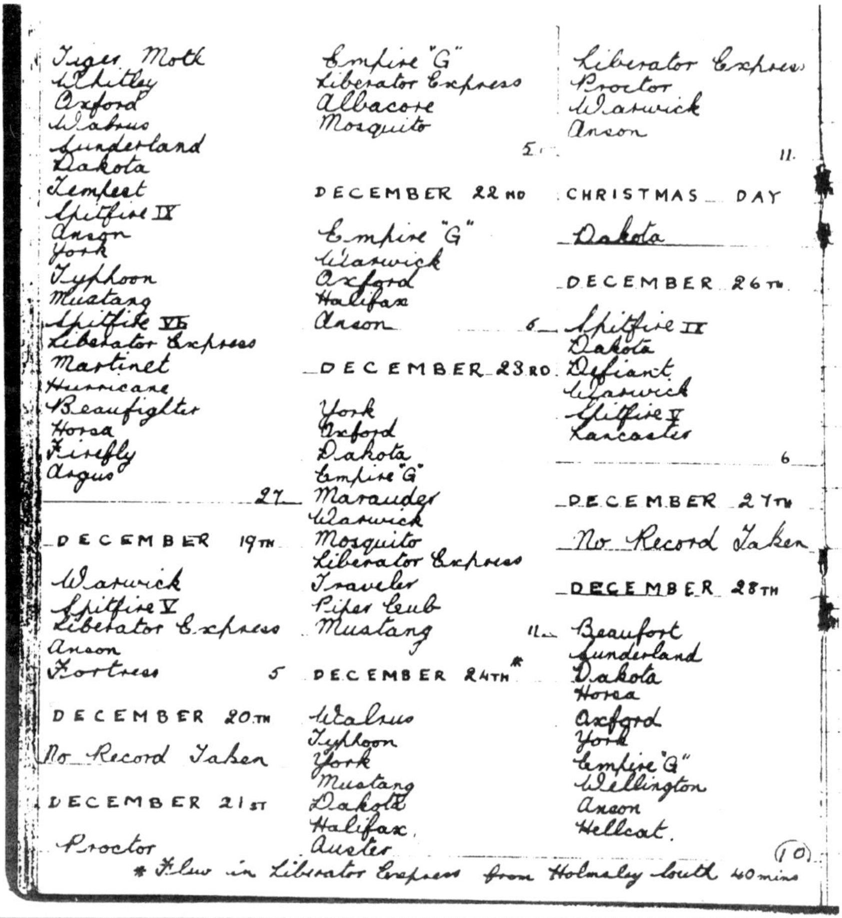
Tiger Moth
Whitley
Oxford
Walrus
Sunderland
Dakota
Tempest
Spitfire IX
Anson
York
Typhoon
Mustang
Spitfire VII
Liberator Express
Martinet
Hurricane
Beaufighter
Horsa
Firefly
Argus
27

DECEMBER 19TH

Warwick
Spitfire V
Liberator Express
Anson
Fortress
5

DECEMBER 20TH

No Record Taken

DECEMBER 21ST

Proctor

Empire "G"
Liberator Express
Albacore
Mosquito
5

DECEMBER 22ND

Empire "G"
Warwick
Oxford
Halifax
Anson
6

DECEMBER 23RD

York
Oxford
Dakota
Empire "G"
Marauder
Warwick
Mosquito
Liberator Express
Traveler
Piper Cub
Mustang
11

DECEMBER 24TH*

Walrus
Typhoon
York
Mustang
Dakota
Halifax
Auster

Liberator Express
Proctor
Warwick
Anson
11

CHRISTMAS DAY

Dakota

DECEMBER 26TH

Spitfire IX
Dakota
Defiant
Warwick
Spitfire V
Lancaster
6

DECEMBER 27TH

No Record Taken

DECEMBER 28TH

Beaufort
Sunderland
Dakota
Horsa
Oxford
York
Empire "G"
Wellington
Anson
Hellcat.
(10)

* Flew in Liberator Express from Holmsley South 40 mins

Daily record of aircraft seen. This extract records the author's first flight 24-12-44

Morse key for the component and using headphones I was able to practice my Morse Code in secret. My sending rate soon became the envy of my A.T.C. pals! This was just another aspect of my ambition to fly whether or not it involved dropping unpleasant things on the enemy and so I worked at it as eagerly as I scanned the pages of my "Spotter" for all the latest "gen". What an enthusiast I was!

The "Widow Makers" only stayed at Holmsley for a few weeks and then followed on to France in the wake of their predecessors. When they left, all the camp rubbish was dumped in the gravel pit at Neacroft. What was junk to them was treasure to an A.T.C. pal, Lou Collins and myself and we had a great time sorting it over. Tools,

FLYING LOG

DATE	AIRCRAFT	TIME		REMARKS
24/12/44	Liberator Express EW612		40	
25/2/45	York		20	Proto type Mk I
25/2/45	York		25	
1/5/45	Dakota		20	
12/5/45	Anson		10	
12/5/45	Commando		45	Qualified Dual 10 mins
19/5/45	Skymaster		10	
21/5/45	Commando	1	24	Glider Towing (Horsa)
21/5/45	Commando	1	30	
3/6/45	Skymaster	1	55	
9/6/45	York 1c		30	

All A.T.C. cadets were issued with a flying and gliding logbook. The above record was taken from the log and luckily survived whilst the original was lost.

cutlery, tins of preserve (each one punctured to prevent re-use), odds and ends of equipment and office furniture all ostensibly buried. We marvelled at the way that jam could be thrown away in such a manner, but the Americans were prodigal in all things and would probably have been horrified to learn how little our jam ration was at that time - almost non-existent! Lou salvaged a long hand-torch of which he was very proud (until the batteries ran out and could not be replaced) and my share of the spoils included a little book entitled “Let God Be Your Co-pilot”. Knowing of the Marauder’s reputation I felt that perhaps it was not inappropriate advice!

“Battle of Britain Day” in 1944 was celebrated by a parade of representatives from all the military and voluntary organisations in New Milton from local Service units to the Brownies. The A.T.C. were of course out in force and assembling in the yard of what is now The Memorial Hall prior to marching through the town and down to the church behind a band. Our attention was drawn to an increasingly loud roar from the North and soon we saw them, forty-nine Skytrains, the equivalent of our Dakotas. In their sand-coloured camouflage with the white stars they groaned over, obviously heavily laden, at about four thousand feet and were gone. I suspect our thoughts were elsewhere as we marched proudly down Old Milton Road; it was not every day we could show off like that! When we fell out near the church we were all treated to a Mars bar off the ration. We must have done well!

And a couple of hours after we had bolted our unaccustomed luxuries several of those mighty transport planes lay in smouldering ruins and many of their human cargoes had reaped the ultimate reward for eight months of intensive training; a moment of glory as they leapt into the. air with their war-cry of "Geronimo!" ringing against the steady beat of the engines and the crackle of exploding flak"; ---- and then death! Holland was not the best place to be an Allied paratrooper that afternoon! Sadly too, many of the Horsa gliders which had started life at Somerford and indeed some which had been salvaged and repaired after Normandy ended their days near a Dutch town, its name hitherto almost unknown to the outside world, but within a few days after such an optimistic start to "Operation Market Garden", a name synonymous with glorious disaster, Arnhem. "Glory, glory, what a hell of a way to die, and he ain't gonna jump no more!" How prophetic the words of the old Red Devils' song proved to be.

Even at that time, Horsas were still being recovered from France. and were occasionally to be seen coming in over the sea behind the faithful old Whitleys, some landing at Somerford and some carrying on inland to 38 Group at Upavon and Netheravon north of Salisbury. In addition, many were recovered but not in a flying condition. These were brought back to Southampton in landing craft and completed the journey to the re-assembly workshops by road.

One afternoon a U.S. Mustang which had been shot up over the continent skimmed in above the coast, jettisoned its teardrop cockpit canopy onto the laundry in Gore Road and made a forced landing in an open field west of Stem Lane. As the pilot stepped from the aircraft unhurt he must have considered himself a very fortunate man; the fuel tanks were dry!

On the afternoon of the 28th October two Grasshopper L.2's landed in this same field. I was at home and two of the local children, knowing my interest, told me what had happened. I cycled off up the lane to find the two pilots looking at a map, obviously unable to tell where they were. They were lost over France they said and had put their light observation planes down to establish their position. When they realised they had crossed the Channel above low cloud they were more than a little surprised! I had completely forgotten this incident until I found the entry of "Grasshopper L.2" logged on that date. One of the Grasshoppers left the next day, but for a reason

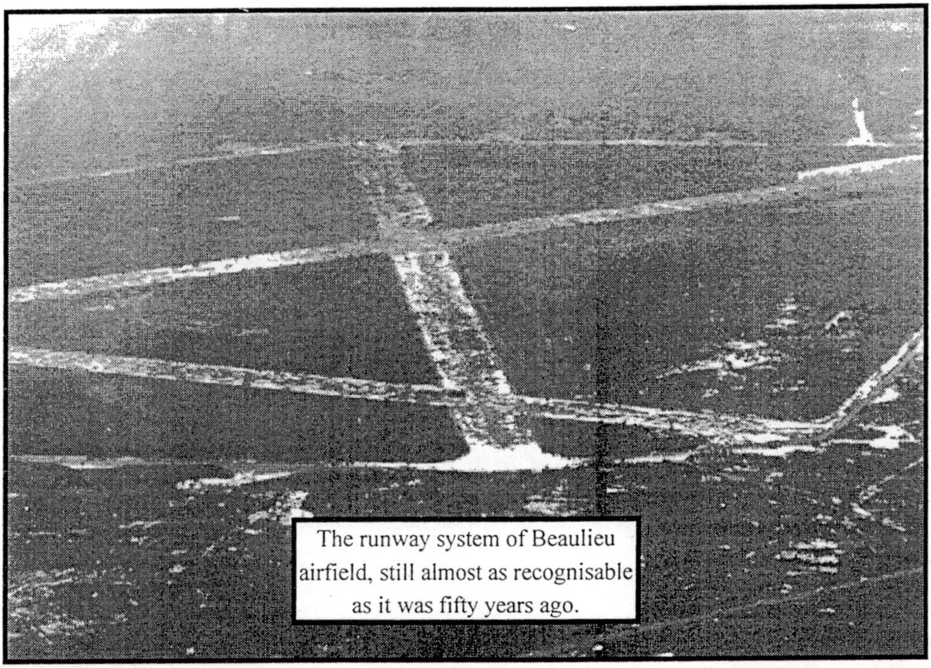

The runway system of Beaulieu airfield, still almost as recognisable as it was fifty years ago.

Pylewell airfield now. The Isle of Wight in right hand background demonstrates it's fine geographical location.

This hut at Holmsley once housed the crash tender I watched as a cadet. It is now used as a cattle shed.

The ex-bomb dump at Winkton. An explosion here in nineteen forty four could have wiped out Bransgore and Sopley.

This Hanger once housed Thuderbolts at Bisterne. Now it is the home of the New Forest Owl

Recycling on a grand scale. Holmsley's runways and hard-standings reduced to rubble for todays building industry.

This sea Vixen proudly stands guard at what was once the Airspeed/De Haviland factory at Somerford.

Bournemouth International Airport once Hurn, pictured on 10 Oct 93. Note the rare Russian visitor TU 34.

unknown to me the other stayed in the corner of the field for some time. As far as I can recall they were the only planes of this type I had ever seen.

Then, early in the winter, R.A.F. Transport Command returned to Holmsley South equipped with Warwicks doing the Italy "Milk Run," a shuttle service with men and equipment. In addition, Yorks and Liberator bombers converted up to the Mark C.6 standard performed longer range duties mostly to India. One Mark 9 purpose built to airline specifications also stayed for a short period. This Mark was something of a departure from the original Liberator design with its twin "zulu shield" fins and rudders. Instead, a truly vast single tail assembly was substituted to improve lateral stability and turned the old "Lib" into something quite different. The V.I.P. flight, part of 24 Squadron at Northolt, operated two or three Liberator Expresses. These were Mark C.7's employing virtually the same interior layout as that used in the Mark 9.

On Christmas Eve 1944 my dreams of getting airborne were realised. Half a dozen of us climbed aboard one of these luxurious airliners and settled down into the rather cramped but well upholstered seats, fastened the seatbelts and waited, hugging our parachute packs. The starters whined and one after another the big radial engines spluttered and coughed into life, blowing out puffs of smoke as the exhausts cleared. Soon we had taxied out from the dispersal and reached the end of the runway. We paused a few seconds. Gradually the engine note became more pronounced and as the volume of noise grew so the aircraft began to shudder. The propellers became a blurr and the tips yellow circles as almost five thousand horsepower strained against the brakes at maximum revs. The engine run completed, the noise and vibration abated and then gradually recommenced as the brakes were eased off and the aircraft started to roll. The lads exchanged rather self-conscious grins (this was a new experience for each of us) and as we roared down the runway and took off into a clear sky, I found myself thinking the song of the U.S. Army Air Corps, "Off we go, into the wild blue yonder ----." My recollection is of a tingling nervous excitement and a euphoric sensation of having achieved an ambition. There seemed to be a symbolic significance in the term "taking off." I really had, and in more ways than one! It was a somewhat bumpy ride and my euphoria soon gave way to a distinct feeling of uneasiness in the region of my stomach; but I was flying at last! Oh, the sheer joy of it! The panoramic view of the countryside from a mile high fascinated me, driving away my nausea and after a thrilling forty minutes I once more set foot on terra firma without having disgraced myself. Not so one of the lads who in his efforts not to give in to the inclinations of his stomach left it too late and to his considerable consternation missed the bag completely!

The sun hung in the crisp afternoon air like a huge crimson ball; I can see it now. The smell of an aircraft of that era, composed of high octane fuel, hot oil, exhaust fumes, hydraulic fluid and all the other indefinable odours still hangs in my nostrils today as I smelled it on that day of days. If ever a sixteen-year old lad had a Christmas present to remember, that was it! What a year it had been; and what a climax!

CHAPTER 6
IMPATIENT ANTICIPATION.

This was a time when my membership of the A.T.C. began to mean more to me than parades, lectures, navigation exercises, morse code, aircraft recognition and the like. We soon discovered that if we presented ourselves at an R.A.F. station, signed in at the guardroom and behaved in a manner becoming to members of His Majesty's Forces we had the run of the airfield, including if we felt peckish, the Airmen's Mess!

Another novelty to us was the Navy, Army and Air Force Institute (N.A.A.F.I.) canteen, remembered for its "Tea Revives You" posters, invariably defaced with a few choice comments! One of the joys of every N.A.A.F.I. was the piano and there must be many fair pianists who first "tickled the ivories" in that situation. Each budding Paderewski saw The Warsaw Concerto, from the Anton Wallbrook film "Dangerous Moonlight" as his (or sometimes her) ultimate challenge and the number of variations on the theme seemed infinite! Nostalgia runs amok even now on the rare occasion when I hear it played.

Ray Middleton had a 350cc. Ariel (I think) motorcycle, Reg Harris a tandem, Ron ("Dingle") Diment an autocycle which had to be pedalled like fury before the engine took over and the rest of us pushbikes, so there was no transport problem when we sallied forth. Normally we went in parties of half a dozen or so and although there was always something of interest to see, flying was the thing. Sometimes a visit to the crew-room or flying control would enable us obtain a "chitty" to go down to the parachute section, grab a "brolly" and then climb into the aircrew truck and speed off to the dispersal.

Almost all these visits were unofficial, but by this stage of the war things had relaxed considerably. Despite the use of the "V" weapons against London and the South-east the risk of any reversal of the general trend was zero. Hitler had ploughed his furrow to the tune of tens of millions of lives, a continent in ruins and the sea-bed littered with thousands of fine ships and aircraft and now, that travesty of the supremely confident Third Reich was being bludgeoned and blasted into inevitable submission.

There could be only one end and it came on 8th May, two days after my first flight in a Dakota. This flight took place at Beaulieu and was remarkable in that I knowingly recognised aeroelasticity, the built-in flexibility of an aerofoil, for the first time. I was amazed at the amount of movement there was in the wing-tips during flight, something I had not encountered in my previous flights in the Liberator and York.

The York referred to was the Mark C.1 prototype denoted by a yellow circle enclosing the letter "P" on the fuselage next to the standard R.A.F. roundels. It formed part of the complement of the A.F.E.E. (Airborne Forces Experimental Establishment) which by that time had moved into Beaulieu. This particular York, as distinct from the standard production model in which I was to fly so often from Holmsley South, had a large hydraulic lift forming part of the fuselage floor which could be lowered to facilitate the loading of items too bulky for the normal method via a roller track into the fuselage doorway.

The day of my first York flight, 25t.h February, I logged thirty different types:- Dakota, Halifax, Horsa, Hamilcar, Bee, Kirby Cadet, Albemarle, Oxford, Blenhiem 4, Warwick, Reliant, Beaufighter, Anson, Spitfire 9, Fortress, Liberator Express, Sunderland, Leopard Moth, Lancaster, Barracuda, Stirling, Avenger, Typhoon, Whitley, Argus, Swordfish, York, Proctor, Wellington and my first "jet" logged as "Gloster Jet". This was before the name Meteor had been released, although they had been in service for several months notably against the "Doodlebugs", "Buzzbombs" or more properly V 1's, which by this time had become part of history.

In the list there appears the name "Bee". This poses a question as I can neither remember what it looked like nor can I find any reference to it in any books I have read. All I can do is to write it off as an aberration.

As I recall, that was the day when my admiration for the female gender went up several points! The reason was that a Stirling landed and the sole crew member was a lady of the Air Transport Auxilliary. No doubt this particular aviatrix was a hardened and experienced flier, but to see about five feet six of femininity emerge from this huge aeroplane came as quite a shock.

The Albemarle was a twin engined glider tug which although being based quite locally had one way or another not been seen often by me. It had a tricycle undercarriage and the rear fuselage was normally left unpropped when it was parked. However, when half a dozen inquisitive young cadets all decide to visit the rear gunner's position at the same time, the point of balance is bound to move swiftly aft. This of course happened and the rear fuselage dropped with a clang! Immediately we turned and went forward again and the aircraft pivoted back to its normal position, but not before the incident had been spotted by a sergeant who left us in no doubt as to what he thought of the A.T.C.!

On 12th May, four days into Peace and again at Beaulieu, I flew on a photographic mission in an Anson. Frank Fisher, one of the lads, was intrigued by a handle just to the rear of the pilot's seat. On enquiring its purpose he was told that it had to be turned to raise the "undercart" and that he could have the honour of performing this important function. He readily accepted the offer but before the wheels were up had begun to regret that he had volunteered for what proved to be a long and arduous task!

The R.A.F. cameraman was photographing a high density parachute drop from a Curtiss Commando, a twin engined transport somewhat like a larger version of the ubiquitous Dakota. Thirty-five fully armed paratroops followed each other very closely from the side-door exits and made a well-grouped landing within the limits set out on the D.Z. (dropping zone) below, situated on the site of the original (1915) Beaulieu Airfield at East Boldre. We were told that this drop constituted some sort of a record being the greatest number of troops to jump at any one time from a single aircraft. The Commando, although employed regularly to carry supplies "over the hump" of the Himalayas from India to China, had not been used to parachute troops operationally until the Rhine crossing a few weeks previously on the 24th March, when the Allied armies with the white stars on their vehicles were fighting their way into Germany in the final phase of the war in Europe. Seventy-two Commandos set out but encountered massive "flak" concentrations on the far side of the river. Only twenty-four returned, one of which was the aircraft at Beaulieu which still bore traces of its encounter with the enemy in the form of several metal patches over shrapnel holes.

When we disembarked from the Anson, we went over to have a look at the Commando, a type none of us had previously seen. The American crew, I think impressed by our interest and enthusiasm, offered to take us up for a ride and of course we did not need asking twice! Having taken off, the co-pilot came back to where we sat on the collapsible canvas seats that lined the aircraft's sides and to our astonishment, produced a pack of cigarettes and handed them around. One of the golden rules of flying was that smoking was "expressly prohibited" in or near any aircraft. (A good old R.A.F. phrase that - well remembered by me as also applying to "promiscuous urination against the wheels of vehicles and aircraft!") On the other hand, if it was good enough for the. "Yanks', it was good enough for us and we puffed away merrily. The two pilots both chewed large cigars.

"Wanna spell up front?" asked the co-pilot and so we took it in turns of about ten minutes each to take over the controls, bursting with pride and excitement. I vividly recall the pilot folding his hands in his lap and saying, "Take it away son, it's all yours." I had previously had experience of a Link Trainer (what today would be called a flight simulator) so that I had some idea of what to do, but in any case he seemed quite casual about the whole thing, nodding or correcting as I climbed, dived and banked very gingerly.

At that time there was a popular little song, "My dreams are getting better all the time." The pilot whistled it over and over as we circled the New Forest not realising I am sure how significant the title words were to me.

Three C54 Skymasters had some time previously taken up residence at Holmsley South in the V.I.P. transport role and a week later when a party of us were again at Beaulieu one of these magnificent airliners landed there. It was a new type to us all and of course we showed considerable interest. We discovered that it was returning to Holmsley that same evening and blatantly cheeked our way on board for a lift home, complete with our bikes, but against regulations, without parachutes. Luckily there were no motorcycles involved. The very tall flight of steps would have prevented us taking them on board.

It was not only my dreams that were getting better! The A.T.C. motto, "Venture Adventure" had taken on a real meaning.

The difference between the airliner version of the Liberator and the ordinary workhorse was incredible. As opposed to the comfortable seating and sound proofing the purely cargo variant, C.6, was nothing but a flying box, the great cavernous interior devoid of anything non-essential to the job in hand. So we sat on our parachute packs on the floor, vibrated and rattled along with everything around us and utterly revelled in the discomfort; although to be honest we did occasionally pass a few lurid comments to maintain our manly images. Sitting in a great Alclad shell, almost deafened, with nothing to hold on to in bumpy conditions may not be everyone's idea of heaven, but to the lads of the A.T.C. it was something approaching it as we roared through the skies. Unlike modern air travellers the altitudes at which we flew were always low enough to be able to appreciate the view, this being all part of the attraction.

The trips were often quite short, a twenty-minute air test perhaps, but occasionally a "cross country" would come up. One I remember well was to Oakington near Cambridge in a York, with a long low approach over acre upon acre of apple orchards.

The most memorable by far took place on the day after Holmsley South had been opened to the public for the first time on the 1945 anniversary of the Battle of Britain. Five of us went up to what was previously the control tower, but had now become Air Traffic Control, saw the duty officer and asked the usual question, "Any chance of a flip today Sir?" 'Yes, there's a Lib. going to Leeming." He gave us the usual authorisation to draw parachutes and we set off with high hopes. Leeming was situated on the Yorkshire moors so we were assured of a long trip. Wizard!

All aboard, the engines started to turn over and then the starboard inner died. A couple of mechanics removed the engine cowling and made some adjustments. The engines were run again, but once more the rogue spluttered and petered out. Off came the cowling again and this time a component was changed after a long wait, during which some speculation took place as to whether we would indeed be going to Yorkshire. But all was well; or nearly. The engine, was fine and we pulled away from the dispersal, reached the end of the runway preparatory to take off and then, to our dismay, performed a 180 degree turn and started back the way we had come.

It transpired that the aircraft had been invaded by visitors the previous day and someone had interfered with the electric circuitry with the result that one of the batteries was unserviceable. After a change of batteries and a few rather undignified suggestions as to what should be done with the person responsible we eventually started our journey.

Having landed safely at Leeming, we were taxiing along the perimeter track when we felt the port wheel drop and gradually sink as we came to a stop. The aircraft had run off the tarmac and was well and truly stuck in the mud. The pilot gunned the engines trying to get free, but all that happened with the starboard brake applied was a mild bucking onto the nose wheel of the tricycle "undercart". Climbing down the ladder we were confronted by the sight of a newly dug drain running alongside the tarmac with the wheel of our steed axle-deep in mire.

A signal was sent to the control tower for assistance and after some time a

Davey Brown tractor driven by a Canadian sergeant arrived. Apparently he had been disturbed in what he was doing and was not pleased. The opinion he offered about someone who could not even drive a plane straight on the ground inferred that the person concerned was a mentally deficient fornicator without the benefit of married parents (amongst other things). We were astounded that a sergeant should address a Flying Officer in such an insubordinate manner, but the Canadians were if anything worse than the Americans in this respect. (Or lack of it!) Anyway, he had the tractor!

After much tugging forward, the only result was to plough the wheel further in, so the tow chain was removed and attached to the rear of the offending wheel which fortunately did the trick. The last we saw of the tractor was a shower of mud from its rear wheels as it left the scene at full speed, doubtless with its driver still muttering expletives.

The amount of time taken by all our misfortunes was considerable and as the weather had started to close down it was decided to stay the night and make the return flight on the following morning. We ventured the opinion (strictly amongst ourselves) that maybe the pilot was not too good in the dark if he had run off the tarmac in daylight. Seriously though, the situation did pose some problems as our parents would he expecting us back; and anyway it was Sunday evening and we all had work in the morning.

A very friendly warrant officer sorted things out however by sending out telegrams, took us off to the bedding store for blankets and found some beds in a spare Nissen hut. Then off we went to the mess for a meal, the size and quality of which was almost beyond belief after our frugal wartime fare! The evening was spent with the Knights of St. John, the Canadian equivalent of our Y.M.C.A. (Leeming was in fact a Canadian station) and being something of a novelty we became minor celebrities for a couple of hours. Canadian "Sweet Caporal" cigarettes were even better than the American brands and one way and another, I believe we were all rather glad that we were stranded.

Take-off the following morning was scheduled for eleven hundred hours, but on the run-up that ------ engine repeated its performance at Holmsley. The trouble was diagnosed as a faulty Bendix starter, but there was no hope of obtaining one at Leeming where the operational type was the Lancaster with Merlin engines. So a signal was sent to Holmsley and eventually a York arrived with a replacement.

The new Bendix duly fitted we took off without more mishaps until somewhere over Northamptonshire, that same engine with the unmentionable adjective started to smoke and then to flame. Immediately the fire was doused by the automatic extinguishers and we relaxed after what had been quite a frightening experience. The propeller was feathered and we carried on with three engines.

Even then our trials were not over. As we came in to the circuit at Holmsley the wheels were lowered in the usual manner, but the "locked down" light refused to come on. The wheels were retracted and lowered three or four times as we made an additional circuit, but the light stubbornly refused to work and so we were instructed to prepare for a belly landing should the undercarriage collapse on touchdown. I can remember sitting on the floor, facing aft, back braced against the cabin bulkhead, head between knees and hands clasped behind head; waiting for the crash, breath anything but normal, eyes screwed shut. The engines throttled back, flaps were extended and we sank lower and lower, the main tyres shrieked as they bit the tarmac and then the aircraft settled onto the nosewheel and we were running smoothly along the runway.

Nobody spoke for a long tune and when we finally alighted and moved far enough away from the plane to have a cigarette, I was shaking so much that I had difficulty in lighting mine. Fortunately, youthful bravado soon took over, but I never told my parents the full story until several years later!

Mrs. Glass, our neighbour regarded me as a reckless young fool and said to my mother, "If I was you Mrs. White, I wouldn't let him go up in them machines." Mother's reply was, "I can't stop him!" How right she was; this was LIVING!

And this was only part of it; I had also started training as a glider pilot at 89 E.G.S. (Elementary Gliding School) at Somerford under the tuition of Flying Officer Ron Hayter whose party piece was to go aloft in a glider and then diving, bomb us with bags of flour. All jolly good adolescent fun, but of course there was a serious side.

The equipment consisted of two or three single seat Kirby Cadet gliders which we maintained ourselves, a stationary winch and a Beaverette recovery vehicle.

The training operation consisted of "ground slides" where the pupil sat safely strapped into the cockpit, the towrope being attached to the glider by a quick-release mechanism. At a given signal, the winch would carefully "take up slack" and then draw the glider along the ground with a man steadying each wingtip until the airflow was sufficiently strong for the pupil to hold level with the joystick. Having mastered the art of keeping level the next step involved using the rudder pedals to maintain a straight course as the glider was winched a little faster to produce a "ground hop" with the ski-like skid under the fuselage lifting a few inches clear of the ground. Then came the "low hop" with again a faster towing speed, this time producing a lift of ten feet or so for around half the length of the towpath. The final straight-line pull required "all out" towing speed. As lift occurred, the pilot would ease back on the joystick to gain the maximum height possible before the angle of the towrope started to pull the nose down. At this point, the pilot pulled the "tit", the rope was released and what happened next was entirely up to him. The approved drill was to select an alighting point immediately ahead and then, keeping the rudder straight gently push the joystick forward and then slightly back until flying straight and level a foot or so above the ground. From this point the glider would sink gradually to earth of its own accord, touch down, slow to a stop and one wing would drop so that its tip rested gently on the turf. The swish of the skid through grass flying a few inches from the ground and then quietly coming to rest is a sensation only to be compared with the exhilaration of being alone in the virtual silence of unpowered flight

Unfortunately, this exciting and challenging activity came to a premature end before attempting my first circuit because of work considerations and to say that I was not pleased would have amounted to considerably more than an understatement. I have had few regrets in life, but not continuing with my gliding is certainly one of them.

On one sad occasion a fleet Air Arm pilot broke his hack in a Kirby by pulling back the joystick on release. Flying speed was lost and in the nose-up attitude the glider stalled into a backslide and crashed, thus demonstrating the folly of thinking you have an engine when you have not!

I had by this time become a corporal and in July '45 went to a week's camp at Henstridge proudly wearing my new stripes. This was my first experience of sleeping under canvas, made all the more memorable by a downpour on the first night which necessitated crawling out of bed to slacken off the guy ropes; not the most pleasant of tasks. However, we all survived to have a first-class week which included my second attempt to pilot an aircraft; but what a difference!

The type concerned on this occasion was a single-engined shoulder-winged four-seater called the Stinson Reliant. Of American origin, but somewhat reminiscent of the Lysander in appearance, it was widely used by the Fleet Air Arm as a communications and general duties "hack".

The main complement of this Naval station tucked away in the Somerset countryside near Templecornbe was the Seafire, but in addition to these and the Reliants there were Corsairs, Fireflies and a type I had not hitherto seen, the Firecrest. This heavy aggressive looking fleet fighter was not proceeded with in its original form, but was developed as the Firebrand in the torpedo and strike role.

One afternoon we were amazed to see what appeared to be a football stuck to the propeller of one of the Reliants. On closer inspection, it turned out to be a swarm of bees! As according to the old rhyme "a swarm of bees in July isn't worth a fly", we felt that a spectacular method of dispersing them would be to start the engine but rather to our disappointment, no-one else shared our feelings.

In addition to the normal runway system at Henstridge, there was an area marked out as the deck of an aircraft carrier for the obvious purpose of practicing deck landings without the hazards of a heaving deck and nowhere to go if there was a mishap. This innovation must have saved vast sums of money and maybe a few lives as well.

In the summer of 1945 the occasional Fortress was observed landing at Somerford. I never found out for certain what they were doing, hut a friend said that they were bringing weary aircrew down to Bournemouth for periods of "R and R" (rest and recuperation) which sounds feasible. At any event, one of these planes skidded on the wet grass as it landed and finished up on its belly with its nose well into Mudeford Lane.

When I went to have a look at it there was no guard, it was completely open and an invitation to souvenir hunters. By that time I had given up collecting bits and pieces, but now rather wish I had not! If only I had photographed this and many other things of interest, it would have provided some real back-up to the text of this book, but of course, photography of that nature was illegal at the time and in any case, film was almost impossible to obtain except on the "black market".

The last major event of 1945 was an N.C.O.'s course at Halton in Buckinghamshire. There I learned a lot about discipline and air navigation, put several squads through their parade ground paces and flew in a Dominie, the service version of the Dragon Rapide passenger biplane. In addition I drank too much beer in one of the many pubs in nearby Wendover, suffered my first major hangover, regretted it bitterly and then repeated the performance the night before we returned home.

B.O.A.C. (British Overseas Airways Corporation) had, sometime before, established a development flight at Hurn. A Lancaster bearing the civil registration G-AGJI with all its armament removed and the gun turrets blanked out was used for various trials and became the forerunner of the Lancastrian, the civil airliner version with its distinctively pointed nose and tail fairing cones. Although nowhere in the field by comparison with contemporary American types such as the Constellation and Skymaster, the Lancastrians did much valuable work opening up new routes in the interim months before the ill-fated Tudors were ready for service.

From a spotter's point of view, these planes, together with the Yorks using Hurn as a maintenance base, were a "gift". In addition to the many Sunderlands, Halifaxes, Dakotas, Austers, Proctors, etc. which were becoming civilianised, they bore large civil registration letters beneath the wings and along the fuselage sides.

This led to a refinement of the art and registration spotting now became the thing. A few registrations from that period, which for some reason have stuck in my mind are as follows:- Lancastrian G-AGLY, South African York ZS-ATS, Taylorcraft Model D G-AFWN, Hornet Moth 2 G-ADUR, New Zealand Sandringham ZK-AMB, Leopard Moth G-ACMN and Junkers 52 G-AHOG wittily caricatured in (I think) "Flight" as a fat pig. This unusual introduction to the civil scene was one of a dozen or so, taken as war reparations and used on internal routes by B.E.A. (British European Airways) as a stop-gap until the introduction of the Viking.

Airspeed had not lagged behind in the race to get into the civil market which had begun to mushroom in 1946. Many new ventures were set up in those transitional times and in the small twin-engined bracket, the old Oxford, now in its civil guise as the Consul with the Cheetah engines replaced by the new and more powerful Alvis Leonides led the field for a time. The conversions were carried out at Portsmouth and the prototype G-AHEF was frequently seen.

In the same way that the Lancasters had become Lancastrians and the Oxfords Consuls, so the Sunderland became the Hythe and the Sandringham, the Halifax (with the addition of an under-belly freight pannier) the Halton, the Anson the Avro 19 and the Auster the Autocrat, whilst the Dominie reverted to its originally designed role with a few modifications and became once again the Dragon Rapide.

In the early part of 1945, my cousin Fred Kettle, mentioned earlier, was an engine fitter working on the successor to the Mosquito, the single seat Hornet which was undergoing acceptance trials for the R.A.F. at Boseombe Down. The test pilot was Wing Commander Cole who by a strange chance was also the owner of a holiday chalet on the Naish Estate at Barton-on-Sea. By an even stranger chance my mother was employed by Mrs. Cole to generally keep an eye on the place while she and her husband were at home in Malmesbury.

Naturally the family link between Mum and Fred soon came to light as did my love of aeroplanes and I looked forward eagerly to the snippets of information about what was happening at Boscombe Down not subject to security eonsiderations.

The next type to be tested was the Grumman Tigercat, a twin-engined naval fighter with a fair turn of speed. I received a message from "Captain" Cole that he would be flying over Christchurch Bay at a certain time and sure enough, right on schedule, the Tigercat arrived and the evidence appears in my record for 21st. March. 1 do not think this particular aircraft lived up to expectations, at least not as far as the fleet Air Arm was concerned as to the best of my knowledge, none were purchased from the Americans.

Tragedy struck one evening in the winter of 1945-6. 1 was indoors preparing to go to a dance when the sound of Merlin engines low overhead suddenly became enveloped in a mighty roaring bang. Racing upstairs to get a view from my bedroom window, I opened the door and the room was faintly lit by a reddish flickering light. I looked out and saw what appeared to be a great ball of fire about a mile distant. Having grown used to the sound of Yorks and Liberators there was no doubt in my mind that a York had crashed.

At that time, the A.T.C. lads were doing quite a lot of night flying and it was on the cards that some of my friends were involved. As it happened, although none of them were on the aircraft, Peter West and Derek Goodall, A.T.C. members of 171 Squadron at Christchurch, both of whom I knew well, were indeed involved. They had been nearby when the crash occurred at Beehive Hill, Beckley and running to the scene, regardless of their own safety, helped rescue the crew.

Their courage was later recognized by the award of the British Empire Medal to these two extraordinary ordinary youths. Sometimes seeing Peter (I do not know what happened to Derek) I have wondered how many people know of this quiet man's bravery. I also wonder whether, given the same circumstances, I would have acted in a similar manner! Sadly I have to relate that he passed away during the preparation of this book

The A.T.C. at Ashley fell into a decline for a few months in early 1946 and then reformed into a somewhat reduced unit. The commanding officer, Mr. Wakefield who had been my headmaster at Ashley Senior School where we trained, being replaced by Flight Lieutenant Collard, ex-aircrew and sometime inmate of the notorious Stalag Luft 3 Prisoner of War camp.

There he was in company with a Highcliffe man whom I knew, Wing Commander Rider, who had two particular claims to fame. One was that he was the first pilot to he shot down defending Great Britain in World War 2 in a battle with a German bomber which also crashed. Trapped in the cockpit of his Spitfire and rapidly being taken to the bottom of the North Sea, he eventually freed himself, was picked up by a trawler and finally awarded the Distinguished flying Cross for his exploit. After being shot down in France some time later, he became a prisoner-of-war.

In the final stages of the conflict when the Allies were rapidly advancing, several P.O.W. camps were emptied and their former occupants herded eastward to avoid them being liberated. The conditions on these so-called death marches were horrific. Virtually without food, medicines or shelter and with no-one, least of all the guards, sure of their destination, almost every participant (or rather survivor) bore a "souvenir" of one sort or another. Mr. Collard's feet were badly affected and almost two years after were giving him considerable trouble.

In the midst of this desperate situation, Edgar Rider was acknowledged by all to have been an unfailing source of inspiration and encouragement, sacrificing everything for his comrades. He duly became one of the very few holders of the Y.M.C.A. Medal.

Another Stalag Luft 3 inmate and at one time Senior British Officer was "Groupie" (Group Captain) Day, my C.O. at Netheravon during my Service days. Also an ex-Spitfire pilot who became a prisoner in the same manner as Edgar Rider, he acted as the technical adviser during the making of the film, "The Battle of Britain".

To return to A.T.C. matters. Our meeting place now became the pavilion behind what was then the Milton Hotel and is now The Speckled Trout and I then received my third stripe and became responsible for training, the part of which I enjoyed most being of course Aircraft Recognition.

There was plenty of flying at Holmsley in Yorks and Liberators and the trip I remember best at this period was one to transport Air Chief Marshal Sir Phillip Joubert to a conference in London. He lived at Barton-on-Sea and apparently often used this mode of transport. But there, I suppose the man who was the chief of Coastal Command during some of the most harrowing times of the U-boat war was deserving of special treatment. In any event, we delivered him to Northolt and I got a few precious minutes at the York's controls on the way home.

I was still leading a very full life, which now included members of the opposite sex. I loved dancing, boozy sing-songs, particularly at the Rydal Hotel and strangely enough had become a regular church-goer.

However, my great love was still anything to do with aeroplanes. I tried for an Aircrew Selection Board, but was unsuccessful. The R.A.F. had, like the A.T.C., entered into a period of contraction, but at that time I felt well equipped to overcome any difficulties which presented themselves and was not deterred by this minor setback. When I was actually in the Service things would be different. Still buoyed up with youthful zest and optimism, I was certain that before long I would be a pilot. I had done my utmost to lay the right foundations and anything less than success would be unthinkable.

As an appropriate footnote to this period Holmsley South closed down a couple of weeks before I left to serve my country.

CHAPTER 7
REALITY.

On 5th December 1946 I entered the R.A.F. My employers, the Ministry of Supply, had offered me a year's deferment but I turned it dawn flat. I passed my medical examination A.1. and could not wait to embark upon Service life. As I kissed my mother "Cheerio" she tried hard, but none too successfully, not to be emotional. My father said, "Keep your bowels open and your flies done up and you won't go far wrong"; we shook hands and I was off to Padgate in Lancashire where I spent a week getting kitted out and cursing the weather which was cold and wet.

From Padgate, home of many miserable memories to many aspiring airmen, we were sent to nearby Burtonwood in transit. The stay there lasted three days.

During the war, this large airfield had been an American reception base for Lightnings which had been stripped down, sectionalised and transported across the Atlantic to Liverpool. Here they were re-assembled, made airworthy, tested and delivered to their units, but as the war state wound down, many were returned and stood stacked up in enormous piles awaiting the scrapman.

Another memory from Burtonwood harks back to the days of the "Yanks". The latrines were nothing more than huge sheds housing rows of "sit-me-downs" without the least vestige of privacy. These conditions provided extreme embarrassment for the modest and plenty of ammunition for the "wits" in our midst. One of the favourite jokes had to do with the American obsession of applying the mass production technique to everything, but I have (perhaps fortunately) forgotten how it went.

So on to West Kirby in the Wirral area of Cheshire for Initial Training in the official jargon, but "square bashing" to all and sundry. In that winter of 1946-7 it snowed nearly every day and the temperature dropped low enough to freeze a cup of tea solid on the shelf above my bed in the billet where I had inadvertently left it overnight. Fuel ran out for the hutted accommodation and the search was on for old cardboard, newspapers and sacks, in fact anything we could lay on the blankets beneath our greatcoats which were spread out and the arms folded in under the straw palliasses. There was no hot water and all the pipes in the ablutions were frozen solid so we had difficulty in shaving and washing. In addition, the toilets were unflushable and this state of affairs provoked much indelicate comment from those of us with a lavatorial sense of humour (99%).

After a few days of this, fuel for the kitchens ran out and the food was almost gone because of the difficulty of transport over the snow filled roads. The day before we were sent home on indefinite leave, I had boiled cod for breakfast, dinner and supper. For some reason, boiled fish, never a favourite dish of mine, seemed to lose what little appeal it already possessed.

All things considered, it would be fair comment to state that my entry into the

Royal Air Force was inauspicious!

Of course the hardships we suffered were trivial when compared with what many had to endure, but that did not stop us from cursing our fate, the food, the weather, the organisation and anything else we could lay our tongues to.

The one saving grace was the unfailing humour which seemed to bubble up in even the worst of situations. True to the traditions of the lower orders of life in the Services most of it ranged between what may be euphemistically referred to as "earthy" and the outright obscene. "Foul" would be a fairly mild description, but nevertheless, there really was an awful lot of laughter!

Another expression of the typical, slightly sardonic Service humour was to be found in what might be liberally termed "music", often parodies of well known songs and sometimes I regret to say, hymns. An example is the following little ditty we used to sing to the tune of "The Mountains of Mourne":-

"They say that West Kirby's a wonderful place.
Though the organisation's a perfect disgrace.
There's corporals and sergeants and flight sergeants too,
With their hands in their pockets and nothing to do.
They stand on the "square" and they bawl and they shout,
About certain things they know nothing about.
And for all that I've learned there I might as well be
Just shovelling soil on the Isle of Capri!"

These words are a modified version of the unprintable ones we sang with such great gusto, but for those so inclined, a little imagination will produce the unexpurgated originals.

To the tune of "Stand up, stand up, for Jesus", the following words were sung:-

"Stand up, stand up for Christ's sake, the C.O.'s coming round.
Dont let him catch you bending, he'll have you on the ground."

Although there were many allusions to homosexuality, it was something of a joke and never once did I encounter or even hear of anything of that nature being taken seriously.

Other "little gems" were merely amusing, for example "My Bonnie".

"My sister lies over the ocean,
My brother lies under the sea,
My father lays on my dear mother,
And that's how they got little me!"

The indefinite leave started with a fifteen hour train journey from Lime Street in Liverpool to Euston with full kit in crowded carriages and corridors and taking turns to be lifted bodily onto the comparative comfort of the luggage rack. After five weeks at home, it ended on the 17th March.

By that time the snow and ice which had enveloped the country for over two months was being replaced by vast areas of floodland as the temperature rose.

Traveiling north through the Midlands was like traversing some alien planet. Gone was the patchwork of greens and browns in the English rural scene and in its place a dirty greyish blanket merging with the murky skies only just above. A depressing prospect indeed.

But all was not gloom. Back at camp there arose a new optimism partly because so much instruction time had been lost and the course had to finish by a specific date. What it meant in real terms was that we had to try and accomplish six weeks work in four; so we were worked hard. Eventually the drilling, the assault courses, firing on the range at Sealand in North Wales and the rest were behind us together with all our hardships.

When we left West Kirby on the 10th April I felt fitter than ever before and I had logged several Junkers 52's which carried the Royal Mail to Ireland; but I was terribly disappointed. All the lads who had stated a preferance for aircrew had been allocated to ground trades; despite all my high hopes, I was now forced to admit that I would never fly an aircraft without signing on for twenty-one years and taking a chance on it or applying for a short service commission which was out of the question.

The bitter truth was that the sudden end to the war in the Far East had left the Service with a substantial surplus of men who had been accepted for aircrew and were now little more than an embarrassment; so the sight of M.T. (Motor Transport) drivers and the like with the white flash in their caps (aircrew selectees) was becoming quite commonplace.

On the last evening in camp we decided to drown our sorrows at the N.A.A.F.I. and consequently became rather the worse for drink. One lad whose name escapes me but whose face I can still clearly remember had carefully cultivated a lovely "Errol Flynn" moustache especially to please his girlfriend. In the ensuing horseplay we shaved half of it off, but by way of reprisal I was forced to suffer the indignity of having a most embarrassing part of my anatomy bootblacked!

West Kirby, an R.A.F. station without an airfield and the poor weather had provided very little for my log of planes seen which I still religiously kept up, but my posting to Number One Ferry Unit at Pershore near Worcester made up for that. I had been classified F.M.A.U.T. (Flight Mechanic (Airframes) Untrained). The training course was at St. Athan in South Wales and I was unable to get on it till July, but in the meantime I had received one of the best postings a "spotter" could wish for. There was another consolation that albeit in an unskilled capacity, I was at last working on aircraft.

This unit handled many of the aircraft being provided to build up the forces of the European countries still licking the wounds of occupation and the following were among the many types which passed through during my stay:- Spitfire, Tempest, Proctor, Buckmaster, Anson, Mosquito, Wellington, Beaufighter, Tiger Moth, Lancaster, Harvard, Hudson, Oxford, Dakota. Most of these aircraft had already been painted in their new colours and national emblems and came to Pershore to await delivery.

There was one very sad aspect of this period. The "Couldn't-care-less attitude" had attacked many of the men who were anxious to return to civilian life. "Roll on death, demob's a failure". was the cry and consequently, "hangar door inspections" where the technician signed for an aircraft inspection without going anywhere near it were not uncommon. I was shocked by this terrible irresponsibility and my pride in the Service I loved took a severe jolt.

On one occasion a ferry pilot died because the engine of his Spitfire had not been checked for oil. A Proctor vanished over the North Sea and a Buckmaster lost its rubber dinghy because the panel covering its stowage above the wing was not secured. These were the more serious incidents, but quite often planes would return because of minor faults.

It was a state of affairs that could not be allowed to continue and things reached the point where one morning, all the servicing crews were paraded before the Station Engineering Officer. His was the eventual and personal responsibility for these matters and he subjected us all to a long and furious tirade that ended in an emotional outburst close to tears. One can imagine that this man, a long-serving officer with a pride in his work and the great traditions of the Service and who had undoubtedly lost many of his comrades to the enemy, was utterly appalled by such a blatant disregard of duty. Things tightened up somewhat after this, but technical charges were still coming forward and morale was at a very low ebb. Unfortunately it was a sign of the times.

Besides the aircraft actually being delivered abroad, their crews had to be brought back and it was the custom for this duty to be carried out by an Anson which occasionally, it was whispered, indulged in a little scent or brandy smuggling. There were no customs or duty as far as this activity was concerned, but at least it did not put lives at risk.

I flew only once at Pershore. A Lancaster was making a return trip to Scampton in Lincolnshire, but soon after take-off an engine fault developed and we returned after only about ten minutes in the air.

An occasional visitor to Pershore was an Aerovan, one of the new specialised small aircraft being produced by Miles Aircraft of Woodley, Reading. It was powered by two Gypsy Queen engines mounted upon a high wing, which brought the large freight compartment as near the ground as that of an ordinary van on the road. Rear loading doors, later to become a feature of many transport types were surmounted by a boom which supported the triple finned tail unit much favoured by Miles in the post-war era. (Other types using this configuration being the Messenger and Marathon). The appearance thus produced made it one of the most distinctive aeroplanes of the time. It was used by a local merchant to import flowers, fruit and vegetables from Jersey and Cornwall.

Unfortunately, this promising little civil aircraft became the victim of the financial problems experienced by its makers who were eventually taken over by Handley Page and only a few examples were constructed.

Strangely enough, what had been the vilest winter that most people could remember, gave way to a glorious spring and summer and I remember well one Saturday afternoon catching the train up to Worcester, climbing to the top of the cathedral tower and gazing out over England in May-time, basking in the sun. The river Severn, content in its tranquillity wandered between fields of green spangled with spring flowers and almost as far as the eye could see blossoming fruit and ornamental trees were in full flush. Below us, the town carried on its normal pursuits and the sounds drifted up as if we stood in some place apart, privileged to observe but not involved. The contrast between the vista laid out before us and the universal gloom of such a short time before was almost unbelievable. This was truly an occasion to remember!

I learned my trade at 4 S. of T.T. (Number Four School of Technical Training) at St. Athan in the relatively flat area of South Wales between the mountains and the sea.

The course was of eighteen weeks duration in which time I managed to log a few aircraft types not previously seen. One of these was the de Havilland Don, an obscure type built, I believe, to a similar specification as the Hawker Henley. No wonder they were obscure. The entire production run of ten aircraft were in one of the hangars and had been, I was told, for several years and were used for ground staff to "vandalise" during the course of their instruction.

The neighbouring R.A.F. station of Llandow was a vast aerodrome and virtually an extension of St. Athan. Its main attraction to me was a large "graveyard" where the remains of many unfortunate aircraft were jumbled together in a great heap of metal. The only time I saw a Blackburn Botha was there. Well that statement is not strictly true; in fact there were several recognisable pieces.

The Botha, regarded with loathing by those who had to fly in it on operations did not have the saving grace of the "Widow Maker". It was a rotten aircraft mainly because it was underpowered, the Hercules engines for which it was designed being needed elsewhere and the proof of this statement lies in its derisory nickname, "The Flying Shithouse". Its operational life as a patrol and torpedo bomber lasted only a few months after which it was relegated to the role of trainer, its function being to train wireless operators in the use of radar and then by mid-1944 it was scrapped.

John Clarke, my good friend of many years, worked as an engine fitter on the Botha during its trainer period at 11 Radio School, Hooton Park. He tells the story of the problems encountered when trying to start the Bristol Perseus engines with which it was eventually equipped. The method of starting was by a Kaufman starter the breech of which contained five cartridges. If the first four failed to explode the engine into life, the standard (though highly unofficial) drill was to stuff a field service cap into the air intake, thus effectively "choking" the engine and almost invariably resulting in success! One wonders how many hats were lost in this manner!

The time of the trainees was not entirely taken up by instruction. Wednesday afternoons were traditionally set aside for sport, but more often than not, details of men were sent off to another area of Llandow with axes. Their job was to reduce brand new

Brigand aircraft to junk! These planes we were informed were the subject of an order placed earlier with the Bristol Aeroplane Company at Filton. Almost before production began they had become, like the potential aircrew, "surplus to requirements", but because the order had been placed it was faithfully fulfilled, the planes in their pristine condition flown across the Bristol Channel, the alcohol removed from the compasses (for obvious reasons), and then left to await the attentions of the wreckers. This terrible sacrifice was enough to make an aeroplane lover weep.

Almost a year of my service had passed by the time I became a fully-fledged "rigger" and training complete, I was posted to RAF Netheravon, still operating the Horsa gliders with Dakota tugs.

I reported to the Station flight for work on my first day. "Just come off the course, eh?" asked a sergeant. "Yes sergeant." "Well, you can forget all that and do it our way." I was a little taken aback but I was soon to learn that the half-whimsical remark contained more than a grain of truth. 53 Squadron were resident at that time, together with 1333 T.S.T.U. (Transport Support Training Unit) and V.I.S.T.R.E. (Visual Inter-Services Training and Research Establishment.) The latter was a small unit operating one Auster 6 and its task was the improvement of camouflaging techniques by literally playing hide and seek with the Army on the wide open spaces of Salisbury Plain.

After a couple of weeks with Station Flight, working on a Tiger Moth, an Oxford and a visiting Auster, I was sent to the Rope Store where the glider tow-ropes were serviced. Though having little in common with what I had learned at St. Athan, I enjoyed my time there.

The section personnel consisted of Flight Sergeant ("Chieffie") Gardner, Corporal Bill Brewer, Corporal Ray Williams, Harry Mountain, "Mac" Mc.Cutcheon, who had been with me at St Athan, and myself. The section transport was a Dodge Three Tonner driven by Chris Shatford ("The Shatford Kid" a "Civvy" old soldier who periodically put the wind up everyone by suddenly going into an attack of malaria.

The job of the rope team was to lay the hemp ropes along the towpath by paying them out from the open rear of the Dodge as it drove forward. Having done this, the "glider end" would be attached to the Horsa (which had previously been towed into position by a Matador lorry), locked and pulled hard to ensure that it was correctly engaged and the "angle dangle" fitted. The tug would then be marshalled into the correct position and the "Dak. end" inserted, locked and tested. The Dakota moved off slowly until the slack was taken up and then zoomed away hauling the glider into the air some time before it too became "unstuck". When the glider pilot wished to land, he would pull the "tit", the rope would disengage and then writhe along behind the tug until it was deposited on the Rope D.Z. (Dropping Zone). The Shatford Kid would drive over, we would leap out of the lorry, attach one end of the rope to the tailboard, pull it straight and then as the lorry reversed, haul it in and coil it neatly on the floor. After a big drop we usually worked four ropes at a time. Recovered, they were taken back to the store, laid out on the inspection bench, looked over and if necessary repaired. Each rope incorporated an interwoven telephone line and a continuity test was carried out after every drop.

On night operations we would usually curl up in the back of the Dodge after take-off and have a snooze on the ropes or sometimes, smoking and drinking that sweet sticky cocoa only found in the Services, tell rude jokes and relate highly coloured and often extremely improbable stories of our encounters with the opposite sex and suchlike. Sometimes on a cold night we would go over to the Airfield Controller's caravan at the end of the runway where they had an electric heater.

On one such occasion a tug, landing lights glaring through the darkness, passed low overhead as it came in to land. Without warning a strange tearing sound arose from outside and the caravan began to lurch and rock in a most alarming manner. Then everything went quiet as the Dakota's engine noise subsided. We opened the door to see what had happened and beheld rolls of barbed wire and fence-posts strewn around everywhere. The Dakota, unknown to its crew had failed to discharge the tow rope and consequently as it whipped and twisted it became entangled in the boundary fence, pulling it up bodily and dragging it along and the caravan with it until it finally broke under the strain. Although it could have resulted in tragedy, the incident caused considerable amusement at the time and earned a nickname for the pilot who had been responsible; "Wirey"!

"When in doubt, sling 'em out." was our byeword for rope inspections although sometimes an effective repair could be carried out by splicing two sound ends together after cutting out the damaged portion or eye-splicing the metal ring of the connector if the damage was near the end of the rope. For those ropes which failed to make the grade there were two alternatives. One was to hacksaw them up in handy lengths and use them as fuel for the heating stoves. The other was to await the visit of a couple of gypsies who had a legitimate business in scrap metal clearance, whip up the unserviceable ropes into the back of their lorry and then have an evening down at the "Dog and Gun", the pub in the village, on the proceeds.

One of the good things about Netheravon was that being an all-grass airfield there was plenty of room to learn to drive the Dodge in our spare moments, trying to unravel the mysteries of double dc-clutching and the like whilst being bombarded with the most derogatory but good natured epithets by The Shatford Kid.

Another piece of adolescent fun we enjoyed immensely was riding on a sledge constructed from a discarded aileron. This was placed at the end of a rope which had to be straightened after dropping. Gripping the end of the rope and trying not to become unseated as the rope was pulled along over the bumpy ground was harder than it looked, as the sledge was not attached to anything!

One of the bad things was connecting the "Dak. end" when the pilot decided to do his pre take-off engine run on a frosty morning; not always we suspected by co-incidence especially when he was seen leaning out of the cabin window and watching with a malevolent grin on his face!

The gliders were, of course, extremely susceptible to high winds and a "Gale

Party" was always rostered. Trying to lash down a heaving Horsa in pouring rain with the ground like a quagmire and the wind gusting and roistering across the wide open plain was one reason why everyone tried to "skive" this duty. No other reason was needed!

There was plenty of "air experience" flying either in the gliders or "Daks" which were also used for parachute and supply dropping. Watching a "stick" of para's jumping through the open door next to me with the slipstream tearing at them as the 'chutes were pulled out by the static line turned my stomach over. What it did to them I had no wish to discover although a night glider descent was hairy enough.

"Tiger" Kelly, a living legend in the Glider Pilot Regiment had survived Arnhem and enjoyed the reputation of being a "mad sod". I found out why when I did my one and only trip with him. Immediately after cast-off the Horsa's nose went down almost vertically and we were literally hanging on the flaps. In total darkness, sprawling in a heap against the cabin bulkhead, myself and the other two passengers held on for dear life. Suddenly the nose lifted and no more than a couple of seconds later, the wheels touched down and we rumbled to a halt. Someone put on a light and "Tiger" poked his head through the cabin door grinning in precisely the same manner as the maniac revvers did. Luckily the enhanced vocabulary we had absorbed from our contact with The Shatford Kid enabled us to express ourselves in a suitable manner!

On the day of R.A.F. Netheravon's annual garden party in June 1948 we lounged in the afternoon sun listening to the Central Band of the Royal Air Force playing selections from "Oklahoma" and other current West End shows. A roar of aero-engines starting up was just audible and as the sound swelled above the music, all our serviceable Dakotas took off in a stream, bound for North Luffenham and then on to the Berlin Airlift.

It was a moment fit for the climax of the corniest Hollywood movie, yet as I watched, it suddenly crossed my mind that what I was witnessing was something utterly typical of the British character; carrying on in the normal way even when world-shattering events were happening around us; something akin to the "Dunkirk Spirit" or the "Business as Usual" signs outside shops blasted in the "Blitz"; even perhaps reflective of Drake finishing his game of bowls as the sails of the Spanish Armada billowed up the Channel.

Patriotism is no longer fashionable, but on that day gazing skywards with a lump in my throat, it was a scenario that stirred my deepest feelings ----- and I was not alone! For all anyone knew at that point in time, the Russians may well have shot these unarmed aircraft out of the skies in a desperate attempt to maintain the embargo they had imposed by closing the corridor between West Germany and the Allied sector of Berlin.

A Lincoln had strayed into Russian airspace a short time previously and had been promptly shot down despite the fact that it was only a few miles outside the corridor so that fears regarding the safety of our transports were not unfounded.

The Dakotas of 1333 T.S.T.U. whose ropes we serviced had the honour of being the first aircraft to participate in the operation (code-named "Plainfare") and it was very satisfying to see D-Dog in which I had flown more than once being loaded as I sat in the Regent Cinema in Christchurch watching the Pathe newsreel a week later.

Without tugs, none of the gliders could fly and we in the Rope Store had to endure several weeks of boredom. I took up cross-country running and thoroughly enjoyed cantering round the area and finishing up splashing through the River Avon, racing up the hill and getting into a shower. Despite this most of the time was spent sitting in the section doing crosswords or trying to find something to occupy us until things finally got back to near normal in the late Autumn.

Flying Officer Williams, one of the Dakota pilots, inadvertently became a hero during the Airlift. Unbeknown to him his aircraft had for some reason been loaded with a York cargo by mistake, and he had flown it into Gatow, the Berlin aerodrome used by the British, complaining that there seemed to be a loss of power and that the plane was heavy on the controls and difficult to fly. No wonder; the load was more than twice the permitted maximum! A Station Parade was called to witness him being awarded the Distinguished Flying Cross.

Most weekends I was able to get a thirty-six or forty-eight hour pass and as Netheravon was only about forty miles from home I was very fortunate. Fortunate too that there were more aircraft to observe locally and a visit to Hurn usually proved worthwhile. A couple of registrations of note were a Danish Larken, OY-DEN and G-ACTF, a Comper Swift which belonged to Ron Clear, George Errington's assistant test pilot on the Ambassador project. An Autocrat registration I remember is G-AHAT.

On the 13th of March, whilst on leave, a Dove G-AHRA, attempting an instrument landing at Hurn in fog, crashed on Chewton Common at Highcliffe near the junction of Lymington and Chewton Common Roads. After taking the top out of a tall conifer tree on the South side of Lymington Road it finally came to rest in a patch of willow trees growing in an abandoned gravel pit. Discussing this accident recently, I learned that the three occupants of the Dove had all lost their lives because, according to rumour, the altimeter was set incorrectly. When I saw the plane it did not look too badly damaged, but despite this I believe it was "written off". I also learned that it was in 1947 and not '48 as I had remembered it!

The findings of the Accident Investigation Branch of the Ministry of Transport (or Civil Aviation depending upon the period) were normally relied upon strongly by the Court of Enquiry which always reported on a crash. Inevitably these findings were seldom incontrovertible as so many factors were involved and one suspects that the conclusion of "pilot error", recorded in numerous instances in the early post-war years, was in fact a tacit admission of ignorance, especially in the cases where the pilot had died and was therefore unable to provide any evidence. Since the invention of the flight recorder, commonly referred to as the "black box", much more information is available. When an aircraft is fitted with one of these remarkable pieces of gadgetry nothing concerned with the actual flight escapes being recorded. Penny and Giles of Christchurch manufacture them and they are exported worldwide.

On 5th. November 1948, bonfire night attained a special significance. Someone suggested making a bonfire to give the Netheravon children a treat and what had started as a modest suggestion finished with the whole of one of the glider graveyards going up in flames. The plywood glued together and finished in doped fabric was tremendously inflammable (or in the current usage, flammable) and the estimated height reached by the flames was about one hundred feet!. Some bonfire!

At intervals of about a month exercises known as "Demons" took place, when the arts learned on the courses were "demon"strated. They were interspersed by an occasional "Mephisto" (big demon) in which other elements of the Airborne Forces were included such as low level pallet dropping and vehicle parachuting by Halifaxes and on one occasion, a single-engined York flypast at around twenty feet. To see this aircraft with a wingspan of a hundred and two feet flying along with three "props" feathered, as steady as the proverbial rock, was really something.

Another technique usually demonstrated by a Dakota and Hadrian glider was the "snatch". This was a way of lifting a glider without the tug landing. It was based upon the message pickup method whereby two "goalposts" were erected with a tow rope, nylon because of its great strength, draped across them, the two ends being joined at the glider connection. The tug would then fly low over the glider trailing a hook which caught in the cable and "snatched" it into the air.

A few days before I was demobbed one of our Horsas had mistaken the artillery range at Larkhill for the airfield, presenting something of a recovery problem when it landed there. The feasibility of a Halifax "snatch" was being debated when I left but its eventual fate remains unknown to me. Some time previously one of our tugs had lost its Horsa near Portsmouth. It landed at Waterlooville but on that occasion the only retrieval method possible was to dismantle and bring it out by road.

My spotting activities were very quiet at this time as with the exception of Boscombe Down, a few miles away, the neighbouring airfields (Upavon and Old Sarum were the others) were only putting up a few light civil types and small gliders. Aircraft passing through so to speak were few and far between.

There had been several wartime airfields in the locality, but by this time they had all ceased to operate. One of these was High Post, situated off the main road between Salisbury and Amesbury. This small grass airfield had an interesting wartime history as in addition to other activities, it was the birthplace of the several hundred Spitfires manufactured locally under the "dispersal" scheme whereby a number of small factories and garages made the components and sub-assemblies which were finally gathered at the main assembly works. This was, in the earlier part of the war, the Wilts and Dorset bus depot in Salisbury. As the war proceeded and production demands increased, this temporary arrangement was replaced by a new factory nearby. From the main assembly the planes were taken by road to High Post and erected and flight tested there.

The High Post Hotel served as the Officers' Mess and for a time the upper portion was used as flying control, but it has long since reverted to its original purpose.

It is an excellent vantage point to observe the flying activities at Boscombe Down.

The Vickers Supermarine Attacker was one of the new generation of jets following the Meteor and Vampire. The first prototype was built at High Post and then taken by road to Boscombe Down for flight testing although the much smaller airfield was in fact used by this aircraft on subsequent occasions. One Attacker, probably flying from Boscombe Down or possibly Chilbolton, dived straight into the ground near Durrington in 1948 creating the most expensive hole on Salisbury Plain! The Attacker could I suppose be regarded as an interim type in that it begat the Swift which at one time held the world speed record. However, it was no mean performer itself and did for some time hold the world closed circuit record. As a point of local interest, this achievement took place over Hampshire, one of the markers being Sway Tower.

Elliots of Newbury, the light glider manufacturers decided to enter the powered aircraft market with the Eon (its name derived from the maker's initials). This was similar in looks to a Proctor fitted with a tricycle undercarriage and it occasionally put in an appearance over the Plain. Unfortunately, like so many aviation enterprises at that time Elliots suffered crippling financial difficulties and the Eon was effectively a non-starter.

I travelled from Netheravon to Kirkham in Lancashire, not far from Padgate where I had entered the Service, for my domobilisation and emerged a civilian once more. In my "Blue Book", the enabling document, my reference for civil employment read, "This airman has been employed in the maintenance of glider tow ropes for over a year and I have no hesitation in recommending him for a similar post in civilian life."

I stared at it in disbelief. I had been unfortunate in the fact that my time in the Service coincided with a low ebb in its fortunes when it contained so many who were reluctant airmen without the spur of war or vocation. My high hopes and ambitions had withered and finally died and this reference was the final insult. Despite this I had by and large enjoyed my service, "gone in a boy and come out a man", and learned a great deal about life.

Apart from the lessons that were inseparable from living away from home and being part of a disciplined organisation, I found that Willi Kwik, a German with whom I struck up a friendship at Pershore, was a really decent chap who, had he been one of the lads instead of a prisoner-of-war, would have become a close friend. He was one of those "poor mothers' sons" who did his duty in the same way that I was doing mine. Undoubtedly there were millions like him, unwilling warriors who purely because of an accident of birth had been sucked into the maelstrom of war.

I also came to learn through living and working with them that coloured men were just the same as us, with the one obvious exception which in those days set them apart in the outside world, but in fact did not matter a damn.

Anyway, it was time to move on and on the 31st January 1949, 3092870 L.A.C. White L.R. became a memory.

CHAPTER 8
COMPLETING THE CIRCLE.

Civilian life found me not servicing ropes but gardening. I decided to turn my back upon what had appeared to be a promising career and revert to the outdoor life of family tradition. In the open air, my own master, I discovered a new way of life, but was still able to persue my hobby of the aeroplane. One of the advantages of outdoor work was that the sky presented me with an open book and across the pages a subtly different story was now being written. Military aircraft were still abundant but now there was a great variety of civil types in evidence as well.

The South Hants Ultra-light Aero Club at Hurn, besides the more traditional planes, possessed the Zaunkoenig. This was a one-off produced as an experiment by German aeronautical students and "liberated" after the war. Its main attribute was its ability to take off and land in an extremely short distance and by its appearance, the Fiesler Storch played an influential part in its design. The ultra-light aircraft were at that time often referred to by their initials, U.L.A. and this particular aircraft bore the registration letters G-ALUA and for that reason I remember it.

Hurn had been officially designated a civil airport in November 1944 and as such fulfilled the role soon to be taken over by Heathrow. The first regular non-stop landplane passenger flights to and from the U.S.A. used Hurn as the British terminal. The Skymaster and Constellation were I believe the first types employed but before long, with Heathrow open, they moved away. Hurn was however still used as a maintenance base for some time by B.O.A.C., the types most in evidence being the York and the Argonaut (Canadair 4) which was a Skymaster re-engined with the Merlin and produced in Canada.

Vickers also created an offshoot there from the parent factory at Weybridge and went into production with the Varsity, the navigational trainer whose design ancestry could be traced back through the Valetta, its civil counterpart the Viking and the Warwick to the Wellington, the Mark T.10 of which it replaced in service. The Valiant initial test programme was also carried out at Hurn after its maiden flight in 1951.

At times when the London airports, Heathrow and Northolt were fog-bound, Hurn was used as the main diversion because of its excellent weather record and on a large number of occasions was packed with aircraft from many different countries. This caused considerable logistic problems, but the coach operators must have made a lot of money and the registration spotters loved it. When the modern navigational and blind landing aids came into being, this traffic diminished, but again, from a spotter's point of view, it was great while it lasted.

At Somerford the main work for some time had been Mosquito modifications for de Havillands. This arrangement required constant liaison between Hatfield, the main D.H. factory, and Somerford, the prototype Dove often being seen in this connection.

On the tenth of July, 1947, the long awaited first flight of G-AGUA, the Airspeed Ambassador had taken place. I had seen the first wooden mock-up in my A.T.C. days and it seemed a terribly long time to actually get the plane airborne, but the pace of its gestation was not fast. Maybe this was because, as a friend said to me recently, the definition of a mock-up is a cross between a muck-up and a cock-up!.

Two prototypes were called for and the development programme suffered a severe setback when the second crash-landed, losing one of its engines in the process. I had watched it passing over Walkford, making its approach to land at Somerford and feared the worst when I heard the thump as it bellied onto the runway. Despite this setback, work went steadily on with this most graceful of airliners and before long they were operating as the "Elizabethan" class with British European Airways.

Two of the most newsworthy crashes of that era involved Ambassadors. One was at Munich where the Manchester United football team was almost wiped out and the other at Heathrow where a landing mishap resulted in considerable damage to airport buildings and parked aircraft in addition to the total loss of the Ambassador.

It was unfortunate that this lovely aircraft, famed for its lack of cabin noise and smoothness of flight failed to reach its expected potential.

There was a proposal to replace the Bristol Centaurus engines with the prop-jet Dart, or alternatively four Napier Naiads, but unlike the Handley Page Herald its contemporary, examples of which still ply between Hurn and Jersey, this failed to come about. A military version, the Ayreshire was contemplated but in the end was not proceeded with.

What really became the competitor was the Viscount. With its four Darts and advanced design, it set new standards in quietness, comfort and economy, capturing for it a never-before-heard-of order for Capital Airlines, a leading domestic operator in the U.S.A.; sixty aircraft. In order to accommodate this gigantic order along with the many lesser ones a new production line was laid down at Hurn in the expanded Vickers factory and this concern soon became one of the leading employers in the area.

The momentum continued with the B.A.C.111 the first flight of which took place in 1963. Disaster struck there as well when the prototype spread itself over a Wiltshire hillside. The crew of six were all killed including the pilot, Mike Lithgow whose name always triggers memories of the Swift. Despite two more crashes during the test programme, this type went on to enjoy a successful career and is still often seen today.

One extraordinary aspect of the 111 story was the arrangement whereby Rumania purchased several of these aircraft in "kit" form for assembly over there. Whole fuselages were swallowed by a Boeing Super Guppy and transported direct!

Handley Page designed the H.P.137 Jetstream in the sixties although in fact it was produced by Scottish Aviation. It was used as a Varsity replacement for training pilots in twin-engined turboprops (or propjets) and also in the civil role, but production was limited. After a gap of several years, one specimen which had for some reason been abandoned in the Arizona desert was brought back to the U.K. and provided the basis for a redesign which was carried out at Hurn. Production was resumed at Prestwick, home of Scottish Aviation and some were purchased by the Fleet Air Aim to replace the Sea Herons which by the late eighties had reached the end of their useful lives. Today they are still in production and likely to remain so for some time to come.

Airwork services Ltd. established the Fleet Requirements Unit soon after the war using civilian pilots and almost every fast naval type must have passed through before the move to Yeovilton in 1972. This busy concern whose function was to provide targeting practice for the radar and guns of the Royal Navy, sometimes as far afield as the Mediterranean, was one of the main activities at Hurn for over twenty years and its departure resulted in a considerable decrease in the number of aircraft movements there.

There has existed since the early post-war days an air link between Hurn and the Channel Islands. Over the years Freighter car and vegetable ferries, Islanders, Trislanders (surpassing even the Harvard in the decibel stakes!), Dragon Rapides, Dart Heralds, Avro 748s, Viscounts, Friendships, Herons, One-Elevens, Argosies and of course the inevitable Dakotas have participated. One interesting enterprise was that of Ian Beesley a Bournemouth fruit and vegetable merchant who for some years around 1970 purchased the entire Alderney tomato crop and used his Islander to fly them into Hurn.

Bath Travel have also used Hurn as the base for their package holiday business as did Kentways who at one period utilised a Spanish registered Coronado for flights to Majorca. This particular type was notorious. As it was taking off, it invariably left four trails of stinking smoke hanging in the air thus earning for itself the most appropriate nickname, "Smokey Joe". Residents in the flight path must have been considerably relieved when this environmentally unfriendly aircraft was superseded.

The Boumemouth Flying Club and many other users, such as Flight Refuelling and the R.A.F. have brought a wide diversity of aircraft types and their fortunes have varied, but Hurn, or to give it its present title of Boumemouth International Airport, despite its many ups and downs, has expanded and generally prospered.

Mike Phipp, under the auspices of the Christchurch branch of the Royal Aeronautical Society has recently written a formal history of Hurn Airport and to those readers interested I can heartily recommend it.

But to return to the post-war scene. The Sandringham, the cleaned up version of the Hythe Class, the civil Sunderland, was often seen plying between Southampton Water and Poole. One of the most luxurious of the post-war types and used mainly on the Eastern and Cape routes by B.O.A.C., it nevertheless was supplanted by land planes and receded with many regrets into the more leisurely past of which it was a part.

The first public demonstration of in-flight jet refuelling took place at Beaulieu aerodrome at the 1949 Battle of Britain display which I attended. The tanker aircraft, a converted Lancaster, trailed a single drogue into which a Meteor slid its probe, a somewhat skilful manoeuvre, but one which was soon to become standard practise. Another highly entertaining item was the "Helicopter Ballet", with Sikorsky R4's demonstrating well the incredible advantage the helicopter enjoyed over fixed-wing types in certain aspects.

I also witnessed on that occasion the finest exhibition of parachuting skill likely to be seen. A sergeant of the Parachute Regiment landed in a marked circle about four feet across. He contacted the earth upright with knees slightly bent and facing the crowd, his highly manoeuvreable blank gore 'chute falling behind him. He straightened, slapped the release and as the harness dropped to the ground, snapped to attention and threw up a superb salute to the front. The applause was tremendous.

I remember watching a Hamilcar X taking off under the power of its two Mercury auxiliary engines, a remarkable achievement. The engines were intended to extend the glider's range for Pacific operations, but the atomic bomb rendered it redundant. Beaulieu too was on the verge of redundancy and this display was in effect its swansong and soon after, this hive of activity became to all intents and purposes a thing of the past although it was not handed back to the Forestry Commission until 1959.

In the early Fifties, twin lads, Brian and Alan Williams were neighbours of mine and both were enamoured of anything aeronautical. Alan occasionally helped me with my work, but the main attraction I am sure was not the work, but the aeroplane talk which always seemed to arise when we were together. I lent him books and recognition material etc. and generally fostered his interest. How pleased I was, years later when I learned that both Alan and Brian had become airline pilots working for Dan Air.

The front page headlines of The Daily Mail on 4th September 1987 read :- "Maniac Terror on Holiday Jet" and goes on to describe how the "maniac" apparently went berserk and attempted to open the aircraft door at 35,000ft. on a flight from Majorca to Stanstead. I quote:- "Captain Alan Williams declared a full emergency and diverted the aircraft (a Boeing 727) to Toulouse in France for an emergency landing." An amusing footnote to the story is that the French police refused to board the aircraft to make an arrest and left it to the passengers to bung the madman down an escape chute with the minimum of ceremony!

The first decade after the cessation of hostilities saw the aircraft industry in a state of flux, seeking solutions impossible to even contemplate before the terrific acceleration in development brought about by the necessities of war. New techniques were devised and countless blind alleys explored, the two most notable of which were the Brabazon seen overhead in October 1949 and the Saro ("Dollar") Princess observed on her maiden flight some months later. By the time these two giants had embarked upon their test programmes, both were white elephants, trapped by the rapid onset of the jet age.

Competitors seeking the same ends often vied with each other in seemingly pointless duplication. One result of this was the number of different types coming off the drawing board and the consequent interest generated amongst enthusiasts who, like me, visited the Farnborough Air Show regularly.

I thrilled to the "Silver Bullet", or more formally the Swift, beating up the runway at 700 m.p.h. only fifty feet from the ground, with Mike Lithgow at the controls. Neville Duke pushed the Hunter to the very limit of compressibility in level flight and then climbed away to return bursting through the Sound Barrier in a shallow dive. I marvelled at Jan Zurakowski, Gloster's incredibly skilful test pilot, making his Meteor (and later the C.F.100) perform seemingly impossible manoeuvres. I stared speechless at the "Flying Bedstead", so aptly named. It looked more like a structure designed by Heath Robinson with scaffold poles the only available material than an aircraft, and yet from this ludicrous start (or so it appeared) came the Harrier "jump-jet", the one class of warplane the Americans with all their resources and technology seem incapable of making.

A great favourite was the superbly sleek, but eventually ill-fated Comet, the world's first jet airliner. As it gracefully showed its paces to the admiring crowd at the hands of "Cat's Eyes" Cunningham of wartime night-fighting fame, no-one suspected that before long, that ill understood phenomenon known as metal fatigue would creep out of the airframe and destroy this marvel of engineering. The route-proving activities of the Comet were much connected with two Highcliffe men, Walter Bennett (pilot) and "Tug" Wilson, (Flight Engineer). Although the Comet was re-designed after extensive testing in a specially constructed pressure chamber at Farnborough and the lessons learned certainly pushed back the frontiers of knowledge in that particular sphere, the delay had proved critical.

Boeing needed no encouragment to exploit the wonderful opportunity this setback afforded them. The 707 was already in production and complementary types in an advanced design stage and by utilising their tremendous production capacity to the full, they had soon captured the lion's share of the world's airliner markets. They have held it ever since.

Ill-fated too was the Comet's stable-mate the D.H. 108 Swallow in which Geoffrey de Havilland had lost his life probing that mystical band of speed at which terrific vibration precedes the breakthrough and the flying controls operate in reverse. Likewise the D.H.110 when John Derry flew it just a little too fast causing it to break up under the irresistible aerodynamic load and shower the spectators with debris on that terrible Saturday afternoon. I walked over the scene of the crash less than twenty-four hours after it occurred and all that remained as evidence was scorched scuffmarks.

At the other end of the speed range, the Scottish Aviation Prestwick Pioneer was a small observation or communications type with a high wing incorporating every lift-enhancing device imaginable. (Maybe the Zaunkoenig had something to do with it; I wonder?) It rose into the air as if by magic only a few yards after commencing its take-off run and landed in a correspondingly short distance. This really was STOL (short take-off and landing). It proved its worth in the Malayan Emergency, operating in and out of jungle clearings inaccessible to conventional planes, and effectively bridged the gap between them and the helicopter.

One of the greatest achievements of the post war period was the building up of the V-Bomber force in the fifties and sixties with Farnborough the showcase. The Valiant, Vulcan and Victor were all four-jet bombers capable of carrying nuclear weapons into the heart of the then U.S.S.R. beside such other roles as conventional bombing for which the Valiant was employed in the Suez Crisis and the Vulcan in the Falklands. Reconnaisance and in-flight refuelling became the Victor's main task.

My strongest memory of the Valiant is one of utter dismay as I helplessly watched this beautiful prototype trailing smoke and disgorging its parachuting crew as it passed almost overhead at Walkford, eventually to crash at Godwinscroft near Bransgore. The test and development programme was being carried on from Vickers' base at Hurn and prior to this disaster the Valiant had been frequently seen in local skies. Luckily, with the exception of the co-pilot, all aboard escaped, although one of the crew had to suffer the indignity of having to wait in a treetop in Hinton Wood Avenue, Highcliffe, until he could be brought down to earth by the local fire brigade!

The Vulcan memory is of an enormous white deltoid accompanied by two diminutive Avro 707's sweeping majestically across the Farnborough skies. The 707's were scale models of the aircraft proper. I think that despite its appealing appearance, the Vulcan must be one of the noisiest aircraft ever flown. The ear-shattering roar of a take-off climb under full power with its mighty Olympus engines tearing the air to shreds has never failed to leave me with a feeling of awe.

The Victor remains in my mind as an in-flight refuelling tanker shearing through a low cloud base with three Harriers connected to the refuelling hoses.

Much of the work which led to this capability was carried out by Flight Refuelling Limited, the company started by Sir Alan Cobham. His pre-war air circus fame had now been transferred to this thriving concern with its factory at Wimborne. Flying trials were carried out at Tarrant Rushton, scene of the impressive D-Day news photograph of the Hamilcars and their Halifax tugs awaiting the order to go.

Many other names bring memories of those exciting times. Some like the Hunter, Seahawk and Canberra became synonymous with excellence, carrying on the tradition of the Spitfire and Mosquito. Others, the Sealand and Sherpa, the stainless steel Bristol 188 and the H.P.R.2 which lost the order race to the Provost have long been mere names faintly remembered, whilst the majority, in their own unspectacular manner have carried the flag of British aviation around the world. Prince and Pembroke, Dove and Devon, Hermes and Hastings, Shackleton, Wessex, Avro748, Beverley, Twin Pioneer, Scimitar, Gnat, Buccaneer, Britannia, Javelin, Venom and many more types of that era still retain the ability to transport me back in time at the mention of a name.

There was something about Farnborough; something unique. It had to do with anticipation, coach journeys, seething crowds, lack of toilets, getting wet through, almost being deafened, aching necks; but most of all the sheer bloody thrill of it all!

Like the rough rides in the Liberators of earlier years, the discomfort only served to heighten the experience. These shows, sometimes in their heyday attracting crowds of two hundred thousand, remain in my memory as a mirror of the post-war aviation scene with all its hopes and disappointments and the occasional successes.

The sound barrier, metal fatigue, transatlantic competition, the worth of the helicopter, prop-jet versus pure jet were just some of the topics hotly debated by myself and air-minded friends of the time, many of whom, like me, were members of the Royal Observer Corps.

The Corps was brought into being as a means of tracking all aircraft passing over the United Kingdom in time of war. The operational set-up consisted of groups of observation posts situated approximately ten miles apart, and covering the whole of the country, connected by telephone landline through the General Post Office system to "Centres", where the information obtained was sifted, processed and delivered to Fighter Command of which the R.O.C. was a part. Personnel were all part-time volunteers, training at local meeting places and then putting their expertise (or otherwise) into practice on exercises when the whole system went into gear as it would in time of war.

I joined in 1952 because of my friendship with Maurie Hack who was Leading Observer, and who incidentally became the Best Man at my wedding the following year. A good friend, he later emigrated to Canada.

The local training venue was a small back room at the Hare and Hounds pub at Sway. On my first evening, my aircraft recognition proved to be the best in the meeting. Training included familiarisation with the table-top grid map, the "instrument" which ostensibly determined the position of the plane under observation, the twenty-four hour clock, the phonetic alphabet, reporting procedures and the like.

Post "George Too", later to become "Easy Wun" and finally "Echo Wun" when the new N.A.T.O. phonetic alphabet arrived, was situated about four hundred yards west of Marlpit Oak cross-roads on the Burley Road. It consisted of a circular dugout, surmounting a small hillock, banked up with earth and covered by two half-moons of planking when not in use; all quite rudimentary. The site today remains as a clump of hollies beside the lane running down towards Longslade Bottom, where the old Brockenhurst to Ringwood railway track, long since made redundant, once existed. Being sited at the highest local point, the all-round view was exceptionally good. The outside ring of the wall, marked off in clock bearings stood at about chest level, enabling the observer to lean onto it, thus steadying his binoculars.

When I first joined, nothing had changed from 1940 and despite the fact that aircraft were travelling at twice the speed, the plotting and reporting remained a fairly long procedure. Spotting the target, lining it up with the instrument which computed its position (depending on observers estimates which were often erroneous) calling up "Centre" on the head and breast set and then reporting the type of plane, bearing, distance, number and height in a stereotyped form took far too long.

Not before time the procedures were streamlined. This meant unlearning the old method and replacing it with the new, a difficult task for someone who had become so used to the original way, that it had developed, like driving a car, into an automatic response action.

I had by this time become Leading Observer with the responsibility of training and operational efficiency of the post, which maintained surveillance over some twenty-five square miles of the southern New Forest. Unlearning the dozen or so personnel their reporting procedures was my biggest headache.

A few memories of this period are still quite vivid in my mind. One is of sighting a formation of twenty or so B.50's (successor to the B.29 Superfortress which finished the war by dropping atomic bombs on Hiroshima and Nagasaki.) These enormous bombers with the tall fin and rudder reminiscent of the Liberator 9 formed the backbone of the U.S.A.F. Strategic Air Command at that time and were based I believe at Marham, a pre-war aerodrome in Norfolk. They were participating, as was the ROC, in a national exercise. I saw them from home travelling south-west in mackerel cloud and leaving contrails; a marvellous sight. I was due to go on duty about an hour afterwards and eagerly anticipated a good spotting afternoon. In the event the only other participating aircraft was a Gannet which made a mock attack on Sopley radar.

On another occasion I plotted a Fairchild Packet in over the coast travelling north at twelve thousand feet. It passed out of my reporting range and was taken over by another post that may well have been Copythorn. There was very little activity so I decided to watch it as far as I could and when it was no more than a speck and about to go completely out of my view, I called up "Centre" for a fix and to my astonishment found it was over Newbury! Conditions were perfect that day but even so, a sighting at almost fifty miles was remarkable.

I suppose the most satisfying plot I ever reported was of an aircraft that was travelling South towards the post and had been plotted as a Swift. I recognised it as the prototype Blackburn N.A.39, which in its developed form became the Buccaneer. I learned later that it was on its third flight from Boscombe Down.

Although originating at Brough in Yorkshire, some of the drawing office work was contracted out to a Bournemouth firm, Saben, Hart and Partners and John Clarke, in civilian life a design draughtsman, worked on the project for some time. His main contribution to the success of this excellent aircraft was in connection with the heat shields surrounding the jet engines. It must have given him tremendous satisfaction as we recently examined that same aircraft XK488 now in the Fleet Air Arm museum at Yeovilton.

A summer afternoon, plotting perhaps a Wayfarer car ferry lumbering up Southampton Water at two thousand feet with the sun shining and the sweetish scent of the heather wafted by a gentle breeze, left little to be desired. On a cold wet night, straining the ears for the sound of aero-engines whilst the rain beat down and the raucous wind gusted across the open forest, it was decidedly less pleasant.

On one such occasion, Cecil Padden our then Chief Observer (whose responsibility was the overall administration of the post) was whistling to himself and I suddenly recognised the tune, "Some Enchanted Evening". We agreed that perhaps it was a little inappropriate in the circumstances!

Some time around 1962 a terrible fate overtook us; terrible indeed to the ardent spotters; we went underground. The aircraft role had by that time been subordinated to the requirements of the nuclear scenario and all but abandoned. Consequently we found ourselves twelve feet below the surface of an innocent looking field off Pitmore Lane at Sway, near the site of the emergency landing ground where I had seen a Harrow and a Battle one Sunday afternoon early in the war.

During the "Cuba Crisis" it appeared that our exercises with simulated bomb bursts might very well become the real thing. The situation, far more desperate than most people realised, brought the R.O.C. to a state where "readiness" was capable of being achieved within a few hours. Code words had been issued, upon the receipt of which by telephone, members would be expected to drop whatever they were doing and report to their posts with a minimum of delay.

For someone like myself with a wife and three young children, it meant an agonising clash of loyalties. I had two alternatives. One was to desert my post and in company with my family, become a puff of gamma-laden dust or maybe die a lingering, horror-ridden death. The other was to do my duty to my country in the hope of achieving some unknown goal and maybe eventually to take my own life because long-term survival was too terrible to contemplate.

To say that I was relieved when the crisis was resolved and the near certainty of a nuclear holocaust averted would be without doubt the biggest understatement of my life. The weight of this responsibility is something I hope I never have to endure again and I thank God I never had to choose between my family and my duty!

Hitherto secret government records recently made public show that Britain's nuclear retaliation fleet of V Bombers were at that time armed, fuelled and ready to go at a moment's notice. It was a very near thing!

On the brighter side of R.O.C. life were the visits to airfields. Normally an annual event, we would coach off to places like Tangmere, Odiham, Thorney Island or Colerne where all the members in that particular part of the country were entertained by the R.A.F. to a flying display and an air experience flight in addition to being able to nose through all the hangars and around the parked aircraft.

At Odiham on one occasion, we were asked if anyone would care to experience a simulated ejection from an aircraft. One of the lads, far braver than I decided he would have a go. We watched with something approaching awe as he climbed aboard the simulator which was a vehicle with a tall (fifty feet?) ladder-like rig mounted behind the seat at a near vertical angle. Above his head was a face shield to which was attached the handle which when pulled, activated the ejector cartridge. He pulled it down sharply as per the drill, there was a loud explosion and he found himself instantaneously propelled to the top of the rig. Rather him than me I thought. He was racked down and when asked how he felt remarked that it was almost a "brown trousers job", (although not in those precise words!)

On a visit to Colerne near Bath I had the marvellous experience of sitting in the cockpit of an Me 262 Schwalbe (Swallow) twin jet fighter and an Me 163 Komet rocket propelled fighter, part of the R.A.F. Luftwaffe collection captured in 1945. I was surprised at the rough workmanship as German equipment I had previously seen and German radio components I had tested at S.R.D.E. were of very high quality.

I expressed my interest to one of the airmen in charge of the museum pieces. He told me that in the final stages of the war when the Fortresses and Liberators of the U.S. Eighth Air Force were roaming the German daylight skies at will, the enemy were hurling their fighters into battle straight off the production lines where normal inspection procedures had been almost abandoned. Much of the labour used was only semi-skilled as were the pilots who flew into action with sometimes as little as twelve hours solo flying experience. As ammunition became scarce, some of the defending planes even flew above the bomber formations and dropped rolls of barbed wire hoping to foul the propeller blades. What success was achieved by this tactic he did not know but it did demonstrate the utterly desperate straits in which the Luftwaffe found itself.

Looking back upon those wartime days, the fighter pilots who immediately spring to mind are "The Few", those courageous young men whose tenacity saved the day in 1940. No less courageous though were these young German fliers, ill fed, short of fuel and ammunition and piloting aircraft, many of which must have been flying coffins, against impossible odds. Again, some poor mothers' sons!

Another event in my Observer days was the annual "Master Test" which consisted of a written question paper covering all aspects of the job and a series of fifty flying shots of various types, some of the Russian ones being rather poor models, shown on the screen of a local cinema. This was the yardstick by which our knowledge was measured and the award of the coveted "Spitfire" arm-badge went to those scoring, if I remember correctly, ninety per cent or more.

There was also an Officers and N.C.O.'s Conference most years at the School of Land/Air Warfare at Old Sarum airfield, just north of Salisbury and on the social side the annual "binge" at Winchester Guildhall for the whole of 3 Group, of which we were a part. On a smaller scale were the"Cluster" meetings where each post in turn would entertain its neighbours.

The aircraft types I flew in with the R.O.C. were Anson, Oxford, Dove, Hastings and Argosy. The latter two were troopers with high density seating: not much fun I'm afraid, particularly the Argosy which literally stunk of aviation fuel all the time we were airborne. At least it provided an excuse for those few unlucky observers who were airsick but it gave me a headache which I was unable to shake off for a couple of days.

Sad to relate, the R.O.C. was no more fun than the Argosy flight now that everything had gone "down the hole". I had served for thirteen years, been awarded the R.O.C. medal and enjoyed myself, but soon came to realise that in the words of the saying, "All good things come to an end".

Soon after I had joined the R.O.C. Queen Elizabeth the Second came to the throne. One of the events organised to celebrate this occasion was the royal review of the fleet at Spithead and of course, the Fleet Air Arm played an important part in the proceedings. Rehearsals for the flypast brought a ninety aircraft formation of Firebrands and Skyraiders across my vision as I stood upon the cliff at Highcliffe and nostalgic memories of nine years before were awakened.

I realised then that I was witnessing the end of an era; and so it proved! In retrospect, this was the point at which the past began to detach itself from a new evolving future, which although slow to disclose its effects nevertheless gradually changed things to the point where I was not only ready but glad to go; so I went.

So what has happened since that sad day? Technological progress has kept up a brisk pace which I have to confess has rather left me behind, but although my interest has lost its intensity to the point where I sometimes see planes I cannot recognise, the basic affection remains. I have now lost the authority I once felt I possessed however and must therefore be content to quietly withdraw from the scene. I have had an enjoyable innings.

Canadians Veterans honour their old comrades at Boldre church yard 1993.

de Haviland V.I.P.s in the early Sea Vixen days DH110 from which it was developed.
Back Row- Car Staham Grinter Moss Grant Warner Clegg Davenport
Front Row- Wilson Barlow Hamilton Gilbertson Cunningham Davis Peters Briggs Withers Jupp Clear

REFLECTIONS.

During the later stages of the war one of the most common sights in the skies, not only here but in every theatre of war, in ever increasing numbers, was the Dakota. Originating as the Douglas D.C.2 in the middle Thirties it set entirely new standards in construction, speed and comfort and in the U.S.A. where domestic air travel was rapidly expanding, quickly became established.

Overseas operators such as K.L.M. Royal Dutch Airlines found the D.C.2 a considerable improvement on their previous equipment and before long its popularity and sales potential prompted the manufacturers to bring about improvements which resulted in the D.C.3. The D.C.3 in turn became militarised as the Skytrain of the U.S. Army Air Corps, and was irreverently nick-named the Goonybird. Before long, the same aircraft joined the R.A.F. as the Dakota.

These rugged versatile planes were produced in their thousands, but in the post-war years the advance of technology demanded a replacement. Many were designed and although some achieved limited success, in its own field the "Dak." has never been completely ousted. Now when most of the replacements have been forgotten, the faithful old workhorse still plods the skies all over the globe. I do not know how many remain, but on the odd occasion when one passes overhead, I doff my metaphorical cap in admiration for a design which can still be a viable business proposition after almost sixty years. I am proud to have been associated with what must surely be the most widely used and universally loved aircraft of all time.

As I have grown older and been able to place my experiences in perspective I have come to realise my good fortune in having such an absorbing and long-lasting interest. Inevitably much of this experience was connected with war, which despite the devastation and misery it caused, still brought out the finest qualities in those brave men of all nations who flew against their enemies in whatever cause. To have watched the trends and developments in aviation over more than half a century has been a fascinating and rewarding part of my life and to have lived through this period of great endeavour is a privilege.

Almost thirty years have passed since I last wore "Air Force Blue" and since that time, Beaulieu, Holmsley South, and Stoney Cross have all reverted to something approaching their natural state, camping sites excepted. Winkton is a fruit farm and Bisterne, Pylewell and Needs Oar Point are open fields.

Somerford has now been completely obliterated by housing and light industry, but at least in this instance,there is a concession to its history; the road names still echo the past. The Runway, Oxford Road, de Havilland Way and Ambassador Close cast the shadows of yore down the years but names such as Catalina Close, Brittania Way etc, seem to have been chosen purely because they perpetuate the names of aircraft; not aircraft associated with those few acres of rather special land.

Am I just being sentimental or would it not have been much more worthy of the days gone by to have named something after the Horsa for instance? One can appreciate that Vampire Crescent or Thunderbolt Alley may have been taking things a little too far; even Mosquito Gardens, no matter how appropriate to the area near the stream, but I feel that a wonderful opportunity has been missed. Little things such as these are the sheet anchors of history.

Thank goodness for the efforts of the Sea Vixen Preservation Society, who have salvaged one of these unusual looking but most effective naval strikers which now stands outside what was once the Airspeed factory in Somerford Road. When I see it, my memories of thirty years ago are sometimes reawakened, I hear again the double bang of "Jock" Elliot bursting through the sound barrier and setting dogs barking and windows rattling and hope there are many others who are grateful, as I am, to the "Preservers".

Hurn of course still yields the odd item of interest, but with a few exceptions such as these, what can I show my grandchildren? Paul, the eldest boy is exactly the age that I was when the Battle of Britain was being fought out in the skies above us. Do his electronic gadgets produce the same thrill as a Spitfire doing the "victory roll"? I think that maybe a "victory roll" to him would be as out of context as his computer games would have been to me in 1940, so maybe it is a case of "to each his own".

Whatever the answer is, one thing is certain. History, unlike time, does not march on, and unless it is recorded, those who walk in our footsteps will be deprived of the opportunity of taking or leaving it as they see fit.

Although I still attend air displays and thrill to the Red Arrows, become misty-eyed as one of the few remaining Fortresses trundles across the scene, feel that same old pride as the "Battle of Britain Flight" passes or mentally shudder as a Tornado blasts down the runway, a subtle change has crept in.

To walk through the hold of a Galaxy as I did recently in Bermuda, knowing that the first hesitant flight by Orville Wright could have taken place within its confines almost passes belief. Had the same type of aircraft been available in 1948, three of them could have handled the Berlin Air Lift with ease! Concorde has now become an unremarkable part of the aviation scene, whilst "Jumbos" cleave the skies of the world, relentlessly clocking up millions of passenger miles every hour of the day and night! Likewise with the type of flying I do these days. Where is the adventure in being moved between two points on the surface of the earth in a transportation capsule?

Predictability is the name of the game in 1993 and somehow, in the words of the song, "Things ain't what they used to be"; so I count myself fortunate to have been born when I was. The scene of my latter day adventures now only exists in the realms of nostalgia..........

My final thought is one which has grown in my mind over the years. How fortunate I was not to realise my youthful ambition of bombing the Germans. Had I been a few years older and participated in the inevitable mass slaughter of thousands of the citizens of Hamburg and Dresden, albeit at my country's bidding in the necessity of the hour, a great burden would have been placed upon my conscience. Thank God I escaped!

And even on the day I die,
This thought I must confess,
If I cock one eye at a plane in the sky,
I'll pass in happiness.

---------- THE END ----------

Appendix 1.
NICKNAMES.

Many of the aircraft seen in the skies in the period around World War Two were more often known by their nicknames than by the correct ones. Some were of course straightforward abbreviations such as Cat. (Catalina), Dak. (Dakota), Fort. (Flying Fortress), Lanc. (Lancaster), Lib. (Liberator), Linc. (Lincoln), and Spit. or Spittie. (Spitfire).

The following list includes a few which are bound to be obscure to the uninitiated, so I will do my best to clarify matters.

Albacore	= Applecore.
Anson	= Annie, often Faithful Annie refering to its unsurpassed reliability. This quality became a byeword in its early operations with Coastal Command.
Barracuda	= Flying Christmas Tree. Radar antenna sprouting out all over it made the comparison inevitable.
Botha	= Flying Shithouse. Whilst not universal, this nickname sums up the feelings of many of its early crewmen.
Halifax	= Halibag.
Hampden	= Flying Suitcase. Its deep, very narrow fuselage prompted this nickname to be invented.
Harvard	= Yellow Peril. An affectionate nickname this one, purely on account of its Training Command colour and rasping engine note.
Lysander	= Lizzie.
Magister	= Maggie.
Marauder	= Widow maker. Despite its early reputation, there are several recorded instances of Marauders completing well over one hundred missions.
Meteor	= Meatbox.
Mosquito	= Mossie or Wooden Wonder. Made almost entirely of plywood in order to conserve metal, this type of construction proved to be extremely tough and was capable of absorbing an incredible amount of damage.
Oxford	= Oxbox.
Swordfish	= Stringbag. Held in the highest esteem by its crews and incidentally in full production throughout the war years, this anachronism with its bracing wires between the two wings proved far more effective in action than many "modern" types.
Thunderbolt	= Thunderbaby. Early models were sometimes referred to as Razorbacks.
Tiger Moth	= Tiggie.
Typhoon	= Tiffy or Flying Tin Opener. See previous text. Those carrying bombs were sometimes called Bombphoons.
Walrus	= Shagbat. See previous text.
Wellington	= Wimpey. After J. Wellington Wimpey a popular cartoon character of the times.

How much more interesting was the nomenclature of that period of history than the unimaginative number labels so often used today; but they were more colourful times.

Appendix 2.
CRASHES.

This list should not be taken as a definitive record of the period and only applies to those incidents of which the author has knowledge. One may well wonder at the number of crashes being so few when placed against the huge number of aircraft movements taking place over the area, particularly in the period preceeding D-Day.

Swordfish	12/3/'40	East of Stem Lane, New Milton. (Now Chatsworth Way.)
Hurricane	11/8/'40.	Fifty Acres, Walkford Farm, New Milton.(See text.)
Me. 109	15/10/'40.	Everton, Nr. Lymington.
Ju. 88	21/10/'40.	Hordle Cliffs, Nr. Lymington.(See text.)
He. 111	7/'41	Pilley, Nr. Lymington.(See text.)
Liberator	7/11/'42.	Boldre, Nr. Lymington.(Taking off from Beaulieu. Full load of depth charges. Exploded on impact.)
Oxford	?/'42.	Marley Avenue Copse, New Milton.(See text.)
Lightning	?/'42.	Fordingbridge.(See text.)
Halifax.	24/1/'43.	Wimborne.(Holmsley South aircraft, crew buried Bransgore.)
Halifax.	16/5/'43.	Burnt House Lane, Bransgore.(see text.)
Wellington and Halifax	13/8/'43	Sway. Collision. (See text.)
Ju. 188	18/4/'44.	Near Lymington.(See text.)
Thunderbolt	Summer '44	(D-Day period.) Bransgore.
Mosquito	Summer '44	Holmsley South. (See text.)
Mustang	Summor '44	Stem Lane New Milton. (See text.)
Thunderbolt	Summer '44	Highcliffe .(See text.)
Thunderbolts	Summer '44	Somerford. (See text.)
Typhoon	Summer '44	Parley Lane, Hurn. (Hit tree.)
Barracuda	'56?	Christchurch Harbour.
Fortress	15/7/'45.	Somerford. (See text.)
York	29/12/'45	Beehive Hill, New Milton. (See text.)
Dove	13/3/'47	Chewton Common, Highcliffe .(See text.)
Ambassador	Not known.	Somerford.(See text.)
Valiant	12/1/'52	Godwinscroft, Bransgore. (See text.)
Sea Venom	11/5/'54.	Hurn. (Failed to take off.)
Proctor	20/5/'58.	Hurn (Engine failure. Crashed on approach.)
Brittania.	24/12/'58.	Winkton, Nr. Christchurch. (Taking off from Hurn.)

And those unknown to the author..........

ACKNOWLEDGEMENTS.

My thanks are due to many people for their assistance in the preparation of this book. My son Steve must have the prime placing for without his technical abilities, help and encouragement it is extremely doubtful if the project would ever have got off the ground. (No pun intended.)

Rob Sawyer provided the initial impetus and has also supplied many helpful suggestions. Rob Stevenson, John Clark, John Clarke, Tim Donovan, Brian Leonard, John King and Don Turner have read drafts and provided useful criticisms, Sue Laird has proof read and the members of Lymington Writers Circle have endured some of my readings and helped in various ways.

In addition the map and pictures of the first New Milton bombing were originally donated to the Trustees of the New Milton Memorial Centre by Mr. G. W. Lane who ran a dental practise in Station Road in 1940 and I am most grateful for their permission to reproduce them. John Woolcot has been good enough to loan me some books containing technical information.

The persons whose names appear in the text are of great importance, for without them the story would have lacked a vital dimension. I hope that if any of them should chance to read it they will not take exception. I thank them and the many others whose experience has touched mine in this context for enriching my life.

LESLIE R. WHITE. WALKFORD, CHRISTCHURCH. 10/8/93.

Paradise regained. The author in Cessna 172 10 October 1993.